SCOT McKNIGHT

A COMMUNITY

CALLED

ATONEMENT

ABINGDON PRESS
Nashville

A COMMUNITY CALLED ATONEMENT

This book is printed on recycled, acid-free paper.

Library of Congress Cataloging-in-Publication Data

McKnight, Scot.
  A community called atonement / by Scot McKnight.
    p. cm.—(Living theology ; 1)
  ISBN-13: 978-0-687-64554-1 (pbk. : alk. paper)
  1. Mission of the church.   2. Atonement.   I. Title.
  BV601.8.M39 2007
  232'.3—dc22

                                                                    2007003736

All scripture quotations unless noted otherwise are taken from the *New Revised Standard Version of the Bible*, copyright 1989, by the Division of Christian Education of the National Council of the Churches of Christ in the United States of America. Used by permission. All rights reserved.

08 09 10 11 12 13 14 15 16—10 9 8 7 6 5 4
MANUFACTURED IN THE UNITED STATES OF AMERICA

A COMMUNITY
CALLED
ATONEMENT

More praise for *A Community Called Atonement*:

"Scot McKnight provides just the right balance between clear, biblical scholarship and accessible, pastoral insight. *A Community Called Atonement* proposes a model for understanding (and experiencing) reconciliation with God and our neighbors that emphasizes the process of becoming identified and incorporated within the 'kingdom of God.' The book will prove immensely helpful for pastors and laypersons struggling with the meaning and relevance of the gospel in postmodern culture. Highly recommended!"
—F. LeRon Shults, Professor of Systematic Theology, Agder University, Institute of Theology and Philosophy

"Traditional discussions of the atonement have tended to focus (too) narrowly on the meaning of the death of Christ. As the title of this book suggests, Scot McKnight adopts a more comprehensive approach. Here is a fresh synthesis of biblical and theological materials that invites us to think broadly about the atonement as rooted in the nature of the triune God, centered in the death and resurrection of Jesus, and extended by the Spirit in the reconciled (and reconciling) community. This is a book to read and recommend."
—David G. Dunbar, President, Biblical Theological Seminary

Connect and keep talking at
Scot McKnight's blog
(www.jesuscreed.org)

and

the Emergent Village website
(www.emergentvillage.org)

emergent
village

For my North Park colleagues

Boaz Johnson, Brad Nassif, and Joel Willitts

Almighty God, who has given your only Son to be unto us both a sacrifice for sin, and also an example of godly life: Give us grace to receive thankfully the fruits of his redeeming work, and to follow daily in the blessed steps of his most holy life; through Jesus Christ our Lord, who lives and reigns with you and the Holy Spirit, one God, now and for ever. Amen.†

The Book of Common Prayer
Contemporary Collect Proper 15

For the authors of the New Testament, the death of Jesus of Nazareth was the "anomaly" that threatened allegiance to whatever language- and thought-forms they may have inherited, and that required a new model, or "paradigm," by which to see themselves, to see others, and to see God.
Roy Harrisville[1]

Jesus was, in his divinely mandated (i.e., promised, anointed, messianic) prophethood, priesthood, and kingship, the bearer of a new possibility of human, social, and therefore political relationships.
John Howard Yoder[2]

CONTENTS

PART ONE
Atonement and Convergence: Where to Begin?

PART TWO
Atonement and Image: With Which Image?

PART THREE
Atonement as Story: Whose Story?

PART FOUR
Atonement as Praxis: Who Does Atonement?

INTRODUCTION TO LIVING THEOLOGY

Tony Jones, Series Editor

I know a lot of theologians, and I don't know one who wants to hide theology under a bushel. No, they want to let it shine. But far too often, the best theology is hidden under a bushel of academic jargon and myriad footnotes. Such is the life of many a professor.

But in Emergent Village, we've always wanted to talk about the best theology around, and to do it in ways that are approachable for many people. Therefore, it makes a lot of sense for us to partner with our friends at Abingdon Press to produce a series of books of approachable theology—of "living theology."

Our friends who are writing in this series have academic chops: they can write the four-hundred-page monograph with eight hundred footnotes. But that's not what we've asked them to do. Instead, we've asked them to write something they're passionate about, something that they think the rest of the church should be passionate about, too.

The result, we hope, is a series that will provoke conversation around ideas that matter to the Christian faith. We expect these books to be useful in church small groups and seminary classrooms and Emergent Village cohorts (our local incarnation). Likely, they'll raise as many questions as they answer.

And, in so doing, these books will not only tackle theological issues, they'll also promote a way of doing theology—one that is conversational, collegial, and winsome. Those of us who are involved in this series hold our own convictions, but we do so with enough humility to let contrary opinions shape us, too.

It's a messy endeavor, theology. But it's also fun and, in my experience, uniquely rewarding. So we offer this series to Christ's church, with a prayer that it will draw many closer to God and further down the journey of faith.

Grace and Peace.

PREFACE

I am grateful to Tony Jones, general editor of this series, for inviting me to write this volume. My gratitude extends to Tony's tireless efforts to get Christians from all corners of the emerging church conversation to gather together to seek unity and reconciliation. The emerging cohorts at Nashville and Atlanta offered comments on the manuscript, and I offer my appreciation for their suggestions. Tim West at Abingdon meticulously edited this text. I wish also to register gratitude to friends and colleagues who have read portions or all of this book or who have had conversations with me, and have somehow helped me come to terms with this great topic: Brad Nassif, Bob Robinson, Greg Clark, Jay Phelan, Doug Moo, Nick Perrin, Klyne Snodgrass, John Franke, Mike Bird, John Raymond, and especially my friend Dave Dunbar.

Because of the nature of my writing, it would be unforgivable for me not to express thanks to readers of my blog (www.jesuscreed.org) who gather daily from all over the globe, who do not have to have Ph.D.'s to be welcomed into the conversation, and who have asked me enough questions about atonement to make me know that this book is better because of them. Long live County Blogdom!

In the last year or two I have spoken at many colleges and seminaries, and I wish to express my thanks to Northwestern College (St. Paul, MN), Crossroads College (Rochester, MN), Grand Rapids Theological Seminary, and Westminster Theological Seminary (Philadelphia) for the invitations to speak about atonement. I cannot thank enough North Park University's kindness to me nor forget the fellowship we experience—Boaz, Brad, and Joel—in our Biblical and Theological Studies Department.

As always, everything I write owes its tranquility to Kris. I hope we will enjoy talking about atonement for the rest of our life together.

PROLOGUE

At a dinner table one night a companion asked me which of my golf clubs was my favorite. I had never been asked that question, and it struck me as odd. My answer went something like this. When I'm at 150 yards, I like to "knock down" my 7-iron. When I'm at 200 yards and there is no wind, I like my 3-iron. When I'm on the tee box, if the fairway is open, I like my driver. On the green, I like my putter. When I'm in the bunker around a green, I like my sand wedge. When I'm at 80 yards and in the fairway, I like my lob wedge. So, I said to him, I don't have a favorite club. I use all fourteen clubs in my bag.

But I once played with a man who did have a favorite club. And it was the only club he carried. That solitary club had to be adjusted so that it could be flat like a putter and angled like irons. The reason he had only one club was that, in his own words, "I'm too lazy to carry a bag of clubs." You can guess that he wasn't a very good golfer, but I must admit that he did pretty well for being a "one-clubber."

This story illustrates the central metaphor in this book about atonement. Some atonement theories today are "one-club" theories that have to be adjusted each time one plays "the atonement game." This is unfortunate because we have a big bag of images in our Bible and we need to pull each from the bag if we are to play out the fulsomeness of the redemptive work of God.

The game of atonement requires that players understand the value of each club as well as the effort needed to carry a bag big enough and defined enough so that one knows where each club fits in that bag.

What does each club in our bag offer us, are we using all the clubs in our bag, and is there a bag defined enough to know where to place each of those clubs? Those are the questions I intend to answer in *A Community Called Atonement*.

CHAPTER
ONE

ATONEMENT:
THE QUESTION, A STORY,
AND OUR CHOICE

In the Christian faith the key to the puzzle is the work of Jesus Christ. Once we have a solid grasp of the meaning of his work, the rest of the faith falls together around it. When I discovered the universal and cosmic nature of Christ, I was given the key to a Christian way of viewing the whole world, a key that unlocked the door to a rich storehouse of spiritual treasures.

Robert Webber[1]

Christians believe that God really did atone for sins in Jesus Christ and that God really did redemptively create restored relationships with God, with self, with others, and with the world. Christians believe that this all took place in the life, death, and resurrection of Jesus Christ and (the silent part of the story) in the gift of the Holy Spirit. The atonement, in other words, is the good news of Christianity—it is our gospel. It explains how that gospel works.

The bad news, the anti-gospel as it were, is that the claim Christians make for the atonement is not making enough difference in the real lives of enough Christians to show up in statistics as compelling proof of what the apostle Paul called the "truth of the gospel." Does this new relationship with God really transform the individual? Does this work of Christ and the Spirit to forgive sins and empower Christians make them forgiving people or morally empowered people? Does the claim of the gospel extend to what can be observed in the concrete realities of those who claim to be its beneficiaries?

The Question: Does Atonement Work?

The challenge of the atonement is this: Does atonement work? Are Christians any better than anyone else in their relationship with God, self, others, and the world? Is there not a claim that atonement generates a multifaceted healing of the person so that Christians ought to love God and love others, so that Christians ought to be different? Even a little? And I'm not talking about individuals, for it is all too easy to find a bad Christian and a good Muslim or Buddhist and say, "Christianity doesn't work but Islam and Buddhism do!" We need to think of the big picture: Are Christians—taken as a whole—more loving people? Are they more forgiving? Are they more just? Are they more peaceful? Are they really better?

I teach a generation of students that believes the credibility of the Christian faith is determined by claiming a confident (if humble) "Yes!" to each of those questions. This generation is tired of an old-fashioned atonement theology that does not make a difference, of an old-fashioned atonement theology that is for individual spiritual formation but not for ecclesial re-formation, and of an old-fashioned atonement theology that does not reconcile humans with humans. This generation of students doesn't think the "I'm not perfect, just forgiven" bumper sticker is either funny or something to be proud of. They believe atonement ought to make a difference in the here and now. Christians, they say, aren't perfect but they ought to be different—at least they ought to be if the atonement works. They think it ought to work.

So do I. If you agree, this book is for you.

Our rethinking of an atonement that works by forming new persons in a new community moves along the trajectory charted by David Bosch, the great South African missiologist whose tragic death is still mourned: "Salvation in Christ is salvation in the context of human society en route to a whole and healed world."[2] If a previous generation was taught that evangelism and social justice were disconnected, even if one could (or even should) flow from the other, the present generation knows of a holistic human being in an interlocking society of connections where any notion of gospel or atonement must be one that is integrated and community-shaped if it is to be called "good news" at all. As God is missional (*missio Dei*) so the work of the church and individual Christians is also missional. To be missional means to participate in the *missio Dei*, the mission of God to redeem this world.

I believe the atonement is good news, and I believe it is because of stories like this one.

A Story: Yes, Atonement Does Work[3]

Dawn Husnick, after some tough years with alcohol, failed personal relationships, and depression, found her feet for the journey. She now works part-time at an ER in the Chicagoland area and gave me the liberty to use her story, a story of how atonement works. It is the story of God's embracing grace that makes a person capable of embracing others with grace so that the atonement begins to work for others.

In my years in the ER, I saw Jesus daily doing His kingdom work in and through a group of His followers. It was a true expression of the church. One day stands out beyond all the others and left me radically changed forever. It was the day I saw Jesus face to face . . .

"Give us hearts as servants" was the song they were singing as I left the church service, heading off for my second twelve-hour shift in a row. Weekends in the ER can be absolutely brutal! I was physically and emotionally spent as I walked up to the employee entrance. The sound of ambulances and an approaching medical helicopter were telltale signs that I would be literally hitting the ground running.

"Dawn . . . can you lock down room 15?" yelled out my charge nurse as I crawled up to the nurse's station. (When someone asked for a lockdown it was usually a psychiatric or combative case.) Two security guards stood outside the room, biceps flexing like bouncers anticipating a drunken brawl. My eyes rolled as I walked past them into the room to set up.

The masked medics arrived with [Name, N.] strapped and restrained to their cart. The hallway cleared with heads turned away in disgust at the smell surrounding them. They entered the room and I could see N. with his feet hung over the edge of the cart covered with plastic bags tightly taped around the ankles. The ER doctor quickly examined N. while we settled him in. The medics rattled off their findings in the background with N. mumbling in harmony right along with them. The smell was overpowering as they uncovered his swollen, mold-encrusted feet. After tucking him in and taking his vital signs, I left the room to tend to my other ten patients-in-waiting.

Returning to the nurse's station, I overheard the other nurses and techs arguing over who would take N. as their patient. In addition to the usual lab work and tests, the doctor had ordered a shower complete with betadine foot scrub, antibiotic ointment, and non-adherent wraps. The charge nurse looked in my direction. "Dawn, will you please take N.? Please? You don't have to do the foot scrub—just give him the sponge in the shower." I agreed and made my way to gather the supplies and waited for the security guard to open up the hazmat shower.

As I waited with N., the numbness of my business was interrupted by an overwhelming sadness. I watched N., restless and mumbling incoherently to himself through his scruff of a beard and 'stache. His eyes were hidden behind his ratted, curly, shoulder-length mane. This poor shell of a man had no one to love him. I wondered about his past and what happened to bring him to this hopelessly empty place? No one in the ER that day really looked

3

at him and no one wanted to touch him. They wanted to ignore him and his broken life. But as much as I tried . . . I could not. I was drawn to him.

The smirking security guards helped me walk him to the shower. As we entered the shower room I set out the shampoo, soaps, and towels like it was a five-star hotel. I felt in my heart that for at least ten minutes, this forgotten man would be treated as a king. I thought for those ten minutes he would see the love of Jesus. I set down the foot sponge and decided that I would do the betadine foot scrub by myself as soon as his shower was finished. I called the stock room for two large basins and a chair.

When N. was finished in the shower I pulled back the curtain and walked him to the "throne" of warmed blankets and the two basins set on the floor. As I knelt at his feet, my heart broke and stomach turned as I gently picked up his swollen rotted feet. Most of his nails were black and curled over the top of his toes. The skin was rough, broken, and oozing pus. Tears streamed down my face while my gloved hands tenderly sponged the brown soap over his wounded feet.

The room was quiet as the once-mocking security guards started to help by handing me towels. As I patted the last foot dry, I looked up and for the first time N.'s eyes looked into mine. For that moment he was alert, aware, and weeping as he quietly said, "Thank you." In that moment, I was the one seeing Jesus. He was there all along, right where he said he would be.

" 'For I was hungry and you gave me food, I was thirsty and you gave me something to drink, I was a stranger and you welcomed me, I was naked and you gave me clothing, I was sick and you took care of me, I was in prison and you visited me. . . .' 'Lord, when was it that we saw you hungry and gave you food, or thirsty and gave you something to drink? And when was it that we saw you a stranger and welcomed you, or naked and gave you clothing? And when was it that we saw you sick or in prison and visited you?' And the king will answer them, 'Truly I tell you, just as you did it to one of the least of these who are members of my family, you did it to me.' " (Matthew 25:35-40)

Dawn's story illustrates that atonement works. It shows that one person, emerging from the community of faith, can missionally spend herself for "the neighbor" who happens to come her way in the effort to bring the reconciling work of God into a new context. Not all see atonement in such big terms; I do, and so has the history of Christian thought.[4]

Now more than ever in the history of mankind, the fullness of atonement is needed. Why? Never has tension between cultures and continents been so high, and never has the reconciling work of atonement been more of an urgent need. Do we offer such reconciliation in our understanding of atonement? My contention is that how we frame atonement will make all the difference for the world.

Our Choice: Which Atonement Theory Will It Be?

About 90 percent of American churches have developed in such a way that about 90 percent of the people in those churches are of the same color. Which is to say that only about 10 percent of churches are integrated. Why might this be so? Michael Emerson and Christian Smith, in their prophetic book *Divided by Faith*, conclude with this: "The processes that generate church growth, internal strength, and vitality in a religious marketplace also internally homogenize and externally divide people. Conversely, the processes intended to promote the inclusion of different peoples also tend to weaken the internal identity, strength, and vitality of volunteer organizations."[5] Ouch!

What these two authors mean by their sociologically shaped term "processes" is what I mean by "gospel" and "atonement" and how we "package" such terms. Here are the dialectical assumptions of this book:

The gospel we preach shapes the kind of churches we create.
The kind of church we have shapes the gospel we preach.

It would be simplistic and colonizing to suggest that power determines everything, but we should be alert to the observation that the power a local church possesses shapes what it offers as gospel and atonement. Could it be that we are not reconciled more in this world—among Christians, within the USA, and between countries—because we have shaped our atonement theories to keep our group the same and others out? I believe the answer to that question is unambiguously yes.

There is no reason to pretend otherwise; it is inescapable. We are shaped by the texts of our sacred tradition but we also shape what we read and hear in those sacred texts. This book hopes that we can learn to deconstruct our readings and our location in the belief that such a deconstruction will empower us to create alternative communities where the fullness of the gospel, and the atonement theory behind it, can be unleashed to do the work God wills. The theory of atonement I offer here will ask many of us to toss away our old bag, add some new clubs, and put them all into an "old bag that still speaks."

Where do we begin when we construct a theory of atonement?

PART ONE

Atonement and Convergence: Where to Begin?

CHAPTER
TWO

WITH JESUS, OF COURSE!

What if Jesus of Nazareth was right—more right, and right in different ways, than we have ever realized?

—Brian McLaren[1]

You might be surprised to find the number of books on atonement that simply do not interact with (or even mention) Jesus' vision of the kingdom. (I'll avoid finger-pointing footnotes.) Why? Because atonement theories have been shaped by the history of atonement theories, and that history has been dominated by Paul's letter to the Romans so one-sidedly that opening the door to the kingdom upsets the entire conversation. (I must add that it is not only dominated by Romans, but also by how some in the church have read Romans—and not all today read Romans that way.)

The kingdom of God, in short compass, is the society in which the will of God is established to transform all of life.[2] The kingdom of God is more than what God is doing "within you" and more than God's personal "dynamic presence"; it is what God is doing in this world *through the community of faith for the redemptive plans of God—including what God is doing in you and me*. It transforms relationship with God, with self, with others, and with the world.

What Jesus meant by "kingdom" opens before us like a bud blooming in what I call the "Lukan thread." Before we get there let me clarify where we are going: we will argue here that atonement is only understood when it is understood as the restoration of humans—in all directions—so that they form a society (the *ecclesia*, the church) wherein God's will is lived out and given freedom to transform all of life. Any theory of atonement that is not an *ecclesial theory of the atonement* is inadequate—and how the Lukan thread unveils that kingdom society is the place to begin any theory of atonement.

Kingdom: The Lukan Thread

I begin with the *Magnificat* (Luke 1:46-55), and I do so for two reasons. First, it is a prophetic word of God that reveals God's redemptive intent and how that intent will work itself out in the son of Mary. Second, Mary nurtured Jesus and passed on a vision like this to her son; reading the Magnificat is (in my guess) reading what Jesus heard as a child from his mother (and father).[3]

Here are some salient points from the Magnificat as they relate to what "kingdom" means: *God* is the "Savior" because he has given Mary a baby, reversing her condition of poverty (in imitation of Hannah). God is merciful to those who fear him (and she considers herself one such fearer of God). Israel's God is now on the verge of "mighty deeds" of two sorts: first, of de-elevating the powerful by scattering the proud and stripping rulers from their powerful positions; and second, of exalting the humble poor (like Mary) by granting them their proper social status and filling them with enough to eat. What any first-century Jew would have heard in these words is not hard to imagine: the Davidic dynasty would once and for all be reestablished. These are words of, if not outright rebellion, at least threat and subversion.[4] And, as if Mary is reshaping the meaning of the Abrahamic covenant, she contends that in this very act of giving her a baby God is remembering his covenant with Abraham.

Mary magnifies the Lord for vindicating her and *for establishing justice* through her son, just as he promised so long ago. For Mary, the Abrahamic covenant is the promise of God not only to be faithful to Israel but also to be faithful to *all* of Israel, including the poor, *so that a society is created in which God's will is established.* She's thrilled to be at the heart of that society. Mary's Magnificat is connected to Zechariah's own song.

Benedictus (Luke 1:67-79). Once again, this song is a prophetic word from God through Zechariah, father of John the Baptist, and a vision of what God is about to do in Israel through Zechariah's son and the Son of God who comes after John. Again, the salient points: *God* is the Savior who is liberating, or ransoming, his people from captivity (think Rome and Herod the Great). God is doing this by raising up a "horn of salvation" from the house of David and that means "salvation from our enemies" (think Rome and Herod the Great). And he is also doing this by acting in mercy (his covenant faithfulness) by remembering his covenant with Abraham.

How so? Once again, by liberating Israel from enemies (think Rome and Herod the Great) so they can serve God (think temple, for Zechariah's concern is the temple) without fear and in holiness and righteousness. And Zechariah knows his boy, *Yohanan* (as he was known to them by name, to us as John the Baptist), will be a prophet and will play a preparatory role in God's redemptive plan of liberation—and this comes about through "forgiveness of sins" (which probably means bringing Israel's long-awaited deliverance and personal transformation) and leading Israel "into the path of peace."

We should not think here simply of personal salvation, as we know it today, but as the act of God in history to ransom Israel from Rome's might and set them free to be the people of God as they are meant to be. If this vision of Zechariah, or Mary for that matter, has anything to do with atonement—and I can't see how it cannot have that as its central theme—then atonement is all about creating a society in which God's will is actualized—on planet earth, in the here and now of Mary and Zechariah.

Atonement, however, is far too often reduced to either an academic discussion about "whose theory is the fairest of them all" or it is shaped entirely into an individualistic acceptance of salvation. But not so for Mary and Zechariah; inspired as they were by God's prophetic Spirit, for them the atoning, kingdom, saving work of God *is* justice and peace and a society wherein God's loving will is lived out. For them, the atoning work of God of wiping away sins had everything to do with God creating a covenant-based community of faith.

With Mary and Zechariah whispering into their sons' ears what God's redemptive work was all about, we cannot at all be surprised by how Jesus states his own mission.

Inaugural sermon (Luke 4:16-21). Packing his best punches for his first public sermon, Jesus embraces and extends the themes of his mother (Mary), his relative (Zechariah), and his own future work. After his baptism and temptation, actions profoundly political as well as personal, Jesus is empowered by the Spirit, returns home, and on "opening Sabbath day" attends synagogue and is asked, in cantor-like fashion, to read Torah. He stands up to read and either picks his own text or finds himself being asked to read on the right day. He reads from Isaiah 61:1-2:

> The Spirit of the Lord is upon me,
>   because he has anointed me
>   to bring good news to the poor.
> He has sent me to proclaim release to the captives
>   and recovery of sight to the blind,

to let the oppressed go free,
to proclaim the year of the Lord's favor.

No one could have better prepared to find the work of God in such a passage. Jesus' words following this reading are as startling as they are full of *chutzpah*: "Today this scripture has been fulfilled in your hearing." In other words, Jesus is saying, "The words I just read are about me and my mission." Which means, to focus again on the salient points, Jesus sees his kingdom mission to be good news for the poor (like his mother and her words) and release for the captives and sight for the blind and liberation for the oppressed—that is, it is the Year of Jubilee!

As with Mary and Zechariah, Jesus maps for his listeners a society in which the will of God against oppression and domination finally finds its way into the fabric of government and in which those who have suffered will rediscover their proper social status. That is, Jesus maps out a society of justice and peace.

Beatitudes (Luke 6:20-26). The Beatitudes are normally *mis*understood as a list of virtues. The Beatitudes, however, are not a virtue list: they are a list of the *kinds of people* in the society Jesus maps for his listeners. Those who are responding to his kingdom vision are the poor and the hungry, those who weep and those who are despised by the powerful—and those who are not responding are the rich, the well fed, the party-prone, and those who are approved by such powerful folks. No, this is not a virtue list but a sociopolitical statement: the work of God in Jesus and through the kingdom is to include the marginalized, to render judgment on the powerful,[5] and to create around the marginalized (with Jesus at the center) an alternative society where things are (finally, by God) put to rights. Here we come into a vision of the kingdom of God on the part of Jesus that is an extension of the Magnificat and the Benedictus and Jesus' inaugural address.

Answer to John the Baptist (Luke 7:21-23). The prophet John the Baptist, staring at his feet and figuring out his future while in prison, sends two of his disciples to Jesus with this question: "Are you the one who is to come, or are we to wait for another?" The question is usually misunderstood: "the one who is to come" is not a title for Messiah but for Elijah, as a careful reading of Malachi 3–4 shows. In essence, John is confused about his own identity, which has been an issue for him since he first appeared in public. One needs merely to read John 1, Mark 9:9-13, and Matthew 11:2-6 to see that John had "identity issues." Jesus didn't, and this is why his answer is not an ambiguous, coded response to John's disciples' ambiguous, coded question. John doesn't ask if Jesus is the Messiah, and Jesus doesn't say, "Well, yes, I am, but I can't say so in so many words, so I'll give you some coded bits you can take back to John and he'll decode and know we are on the same page."

In fact, John misunderstands Jesus and asks if Jesus is "Elijah"—for that would mean judgment and John's release. But Jesus says, "No, in fact, I'm not the 'one who is to come' but someone else. I am the figure mentioned in Isaiah 29:18-19, 35:5-6, and 61:1"—which are the lines Jesus quotes and I will cite immediately. What Jesus tells John's disciples (to tell John) is simple and profoundly revealing of Jesus' mission:

> Go and tell John what you have seen and heard: the blind receive their sight, the lame walk, the lepers are cleansed, the deaf hear, the dead are raised, the poor have good news brought to them. And blessed is anyone who takes no offense at me.

Once again, we return to Mary, to Zechariah, to the inaugural sermon, and to the Beatitudes: Jesus' mission, his vision of the kingdom, is about restoring the blind, giving limber legs to the lame, wiping the skin of the lepers clean, filling the ears of the deaf with music and sounds, bringing back dead people from the grave, and making sure the poor are taken care of by restoring them to their proper social location. The mission of Jesus is healing justice, the ending of disease, dislocation, and oppression. Beyond those conditions, Jesus announces the creation of a covenanted community where the covenant God's will is lived out for each and every person.

We cannot back down from this: if this is Jesus' vision, and atonement is one way of speaking of what God's redemptive work in this world is designed to accomplish, then the creation of a community where God's will is done is inherent to the meaning of atonement. Any discussion of atonement apart from discussion of the kingdom fails to do justice to the biblical framing of God's redemptive work in this world. I make no apologies and I repeat myself for emphasis. Jesus' kingdom vision and atonement are related; separating them is an act of violence. When the many theories of atonement miss this theme, they are missing the telic vision of what atonement is designed to accomplish. Atonement creates the kingdom of God.

Early church (Acts 2:42-47; 4:32-35). The Lukan thread can be followed from the words of Mary right through Zechariah to Jesus' ministry and teachings and Holy Week—in fact, the kingdom is shaped by the "divine necessity" of Jesus' own death, his resurrection vindication, and his sending of the Holy Spirit. When Jesus is transfigured, Luke tells us that Moses and Elijah speak of Jesus' "departure," which translates the Greek word *exodus* (Luke 9:31). The "exodus" death of Jesus leads his followers to freedom, and that freedom is what the kingdom is all about in Luke.

Jesus' kingdom mission, which involved his life, his death, his resurrection, and his sending of the pentecostal Holy Spirit, comes to fruition in Christian community described in Acts 2. Here we see, once again, the *ecclesial* shape of the kingdom and the atoning work of Jesus. That is, the ecclesial shape of the followers of Jesus is an indication of what Jesus was getting at when he continually announced the arrival (or near arrival) of the kingdom of God. That ecclesial community is noted by the following salient items: interpersonal fellowship with the apostles and one another, and interpersonal fellowship with the Lord in the breaking of bread and with God in prayer. Such spiritual "disciplines" emerged into dramatic miracles, an economical availability to and liability for one another, and the obvious growth in numbers of converts to the ecclesial community of faith. In other words, we are witnessing just what Jesus had in mind when he announced his ministry in terms of Isaiah 29, 35, and 61, when he blessed special people groups, and when he announced that God's kingdom work would be the creation of a community in which God's will would be actualized. It is a mistake to connect this ecclesial fellowship with Pentecost only; to be sure, this is the work of God's Spirit, but God's Spirit creates the vision Jesus (and Mary and Zechariah) had declared.

The same can be said for Acts 4:32-35. Here we have a society in which God's will is understood in terms like equality, social justice, economic availability to and liability for one another, and fellowship. Jesus' vision was coming into existence in the growing clutch of Jesus' followers who were experiencing the empowering graces of Pentecost. The church is the alternative society to the structures of power found in the Roman (and Jewish) world. The theme cannot be developed here, but suffice it to say that such a vision of the kingdom of God is clearly a third way.[6]

Back to atonement. I contend that a Christian theory of atonement must begin with how Jesus understands the kingdom. But atonement is complex and there is more than one biblical theme to factor in that kingdom. In the next two chapters I want to examine several more themes that need to be factored in if we are to grasp the fullness of atonement. So, where else do we begin?

CHAPTER
THREE

WITH GOD, WITH EIKONS,
AND WITH SIN, TOO

"Atonement." It is a fine, solid, twelfth-century Middle English word, the kind of word one is inclined to trust. Think of at-one-ment: What was separated is now at one.

—Richard John Neuhaus[1]

Ask any fiction writer how they come up with their stories and they will almost always tell you the same thing: the characters and their lives flow out of the *beginning* of the story. When there are bits in a story that don't flow naturally from the beginning, they are recognizable—as when Mark Twain suddenly finds it necessary to create a vaudeville act on the raft floating down the mighty Mississippi in his (otherwise) splendid *The Adventures of Huckleberry Finn*.

The story of atonement is the same. Everything depends on where you begin. For a variety of reasons, some want to begin with God's wrath. C. S. Lewis discusses such an emphasis in *Mere Christianity* in the chapter "The Perfect Penitent" with these words: "According to that theory God wanted to punish men for having deserted and joined the Great Rebel, but Christ volunteered to be punished instead, and so God let us off."[2] Lewis adds that this theory rarely gets told just like this. My point is that *where we begin* shapes *where we end up*. If you begin with wrath, you get an atonement that tells the story of wrath being pacified.

Others begin elsewhere. The Eastern theologians tend to begin with death, and their story of atonement is essentially God's overcoming death through the gift of immortality in Christ. Most would agree that death is a major focus for Paul's gospel—especially in Romans. But preoccupation with death can become ... well, morbid. Others focus exclusively on the kingdom vision of Jesus, with the result that atonement becomes little more than liberation; few would want to deny the importance of freedom, but atonement is more than that.

So where do we begin? I've already said that I think we have to begin with the kingdom. I am now suggesting that we need to begin at six more places. When each is brought into place, atonement themes converge into one solid core where Christ is all in all. These themes will shape the kind of golf bag that can handle all the clubs.

With God and the *Perichoresis*

In the Fourth Gospel Jesus says, "The Father and I are *one*" (10:30) and then "if I do [the works of the Father], even though you do not believe me, believe the works, so that you may know and understand that the Father is *in* me and I am *in* the Father" (10:38, emphasis added). One of the most profound and penetrating explorations of classical Cappadocian and Eastern theology is how the Father and the Son are *one*. How are they one?

A part of the answer to the question is called the *perichoresis*. *Perichoresis* refers to the mutual interdependence, or further yet, the mutual interpenetration of the persons of the Trinity. Miroslav Volf, a noted theologian at Yale, speaks of the *perichoresis* as the "reciprocal *interiority*" of the persons of the Trinity.[3] *Perichoresis* seeks to articulate both what God is like and how the various persons of the Trinity relate to one another, and the conclusion is that they remain wholly distinct while being wholly interior to one another—so interior that one can say that the Son only *is* in the sense that the Father and the Spirit indwell the Son. According to LeRon Shults, "The point of the doctrine of perichoresis is that in the Trinity, personhood and relation-to-other are not separated as they are in us."[4] The Father and the Son and the Spirit retain genuine separable identities while at the same time they are so related to one another that one can't be known without the other. Relationality, in other words, is inherent to who God is.[5]

The *perichoresis*, or God's essential mutual interiority, defines both love (the interpenetration) and holiness (the sacredness and purity of its interpenetration). The *perichoresis* also establishes what really is. Genuine, final reality for humans is to participate in the reciprocal interiority of the Trinity in Christ through the Spirit, and to extend this interiority to others as an approximation of that *perichoresis*. Genuine reality then is relational; genuine atonement is reconciliation. Such language can sound like nothing more than jargon, so we need to explore this for a moment in the teachings of Jesus.

Nothing less than human participation in the *perichoresis* is in view in what Jesus says in John 17:20-24:

> I ask not only on behalf of these, but also on behalf of those who will believe in me through their word, that they may all be one. As you, Father, are in me and I am in you, *may they also be in us*, so that the world may believe that you have sent me. The glory that you have given me I have given them, *so that they may be one*, as we are one, I in them and you in me, *that they may become completely one*, so that the world may know that you have sent me and have loved them even as you have loved me. Father, I desire that those also, whom you have given me, *may be with me where I am*, to see my glory, which you have given me because you loved me before the foundation of the world. (emphasis added)

Round and round goes John's Gospel: as the Father is in the Son, as the Son is in the Father, so the Son is in us and we are in the Son. And, if we are in the Son, we are in the Father, and if we are in the Son and the Father, then we are designed for mutual interiority to the degree that humans can participate in God.

Union with Christ, being "in Christ," "abiding in Christ," living "in the Spirit," being "conformed" to the image of Christ, "fellowship" with Christ and one another, the "body of Christ" and the "gifts of the Spirit"—these and other metaphors in the Bible are different ways of expressing the absolutely foundational dimension of relationship in the work of God called atonement. Michael Jinkins expresses this idea as he describes his "course" in theology: "The meaning and shape of our life together as a community of persons is grounded in the inner life of God, the Trinity, and has been revealed to us in the life, death and resurrection of Jesus Christ."[6]

Atonement finally concerns union with God and, simultaneously, communion with one another as its mirror among God's created beings. If the *perichoresis* is another place to begin, so also is the central importance of being made in "God's image."

With Humans as Eikons

Theologians normally call human uniqueness *imago Dei* or the "image of God." The expression "image of God" derives from Genesis 1:26-27, where the Hebrew terms *tselem* ("image") and *demut* ("likeness") are used. The Greek translation of the Hebrew *tselem* is *Eikon*, and it is this term that will carry the load in what follows. I speak then of our uniqueness as being made as *Eikons* of God. Once again, and because of the powerful threat to this biblical idea in a post-Darwinian culture, we need to discuss what it means to say humans are Eikons.

The Discussion

The intellectual discussion about human nature, what theologians call the Eikon, or image, of God, continues to fascinate. The discussion begins in the Far East with Confucius's cultured, traditional wisdom. We find another set of ideas in Upanishadic Hinduism's concepts of material and spiritual reality in the terms *Brahman* and *Atman*. In the West we find Plato's tripartite human (*epithumia, nous, psyche*) and the ideal Forms, and in Aristotle we come to a more empirical, earthy concern that *arete* can be habituated in the good citizen by disciplined practice. But however much professors of classical philosophy like Plato and Aristotle, it is Immanuel Kant's version of Plato that paved the path of human nature that most walk on today.

Kant was concerned with the *phenomenal* ("what appears to the senses to all") and the *noumenal* ("what is known by thought"—God and the soul). The latter is the thing-in-itself and the object of pure reason, though he later denied even this could be known. Kant drew a line, a thick one, between the phenomenal and the noumenal, and from his time on the Christian belief that humans are Eikons, which is indiscoverable phenomenologically, was put on the defensive.

This defensive posture was aggravated by Freud's version of Plato—the Id, the Ego, and the Super-Ego—and Darwin's explanation that humans are the complex result of an evolutionary scheme that is still underway. When Kant drew that line, the Christian theory that humans are Eikons was bracketed right off the map. For example, in Steven Pinker's *The Blank Slate*, appropriately subtitled *The Denial of Human Nature*, Pinker seeks physical and scientific explanation for everything about humans—from brain to heart and back to the brain, it is all about the brain.[7] But humans intuit that such explanations are not enough, mostly because they do not describe what humans witness or experience.

The Bible: The Shift from Representation to Redemption

Here's what the Bible says at Genesis 1:26-27:

> Then God said, "Let us make humankind in our image, according to our likeness; and let them have dominion over the fish of the sea, and over the birds of the air, and over the cattle, and over all the wild animals of the earth, and over every creeping thing that creeps upon the earth."
> So God created humankind in his image,
> in the image of God he created them;
> male and female he created them.

Most scholars of the meaning of "Eikon" would agree that it refers to humans *representing* God in this world; humans as Eikons are earth's divine representatives. The expression "image of God" is only found in the Old Testament at Genesis 5:1 and 9:6. Genesis 5:1 rehearses Genesis 1–2 and 9:6 prohibits, rather significantly, murder because humans are Eikons of God. What we learn in the sweep of the biblical story is that the created Eikons of Genesis 1–2, the ones designed by God to represent God in this world, become "cracked" Eikons in Genesis 3, and the rest of human existence is the life of cracked Eikons who do not accomplish their task of ruling in this world as God's representatives.

"Eikon of God" is not found again in the entire Old Testament, though it does appear in noncanonical Jewish texts like Wisdom of Solomon, where it connotes immortality (2:23); in Sirach, where it speaks of governance over creation (17:3); and in 2 Esdras, where it is used to plea that God should be merciful to sinful humans (8:44). What is rarely observed is that the "idols" that God prohibits, say in Exodus 20, are prohibited in part because God has made his own representative "idols": humans as God's Eikons.

As the Bible moves forward into the New Testament, though, "Eikon" morphs; it shifts from denoting a ruling-representative function to a *redemptive* role. There are a number of NT references, but we will limit our discussion to two principal passages: 2 Corinthians 4:3-6 and then 3:17-18.

> And even if our gospel is veiled, it is veiled to those who are perishing. In their case the god of this world has blinded the minds of the unbelievers, to

keep them from seeing the light of the gospel of the glory of *Christ, who is the image of God*. For we do not proclaim ourselves; we proclaim Jesus Christ as Lord and ourselves as your slaves for Jesus' sake. For it is the God who said, "Let light shine out of darkness," who has shone in our hearts to give the light of the knowledge of the glory of God in the face of Jesus Christ. (emphasis added)

Now the Lord is the Spirit, and where the Spirit of the Lord is, there is freedom. And all of us, with unveiled faces, seeing the glory of the Lord as though reflected in a mirror, *are being transformed into the same image from one degree of glory to another*; for this comes from the Lord, the Spirit. (emphasis added)

The work of the Spirit, the apostle Paul tells us, is the ongoing redemptive transformation of the community of Christians into the glorious Eikon of Jesus Christ himself. Paul shifts the emphasis of the word Eikon from the *ruling-representative* human Eikon to the *redeemed* Eikon because he believes Jesus Christ is the perfect God-Man Eikon.

Let me now sum up the biblical understanding of humans as Eikons of God in four stages: humans are created as Eikons, cracked in their present Eikonic struggle, shaped into Christ-like Eikons as they follow Jesus, and destined to be conformed to Christ in union with God and communion with others in eternity.

The Meaning of Eikon

We are now ready to push further. Kant, you will remember, drew that thick line between the phenomenal and the noumenal, and this put theologians on the defensive: somehow, they thought, we should demonstrate the legitimacy of "Eikon" through examination of the phenomenal. To do this, theologians learned to define the Eikon *by comparing it to the rest of creation*. Those who have focused on Eikon by comparing it to the rest of creation come to these sorts of conclusions: humans have superior intelligence, they have relational capacities (Karl Barth), they are spiritual (the Reformers), they are self-conscious (N. Berdyaev), they are moral beings (Christian Smith), and the list of what makes humans special or superior goes on.

Suggesting that these folks are missing something, as I am doing now, might draw even the attention of Zeus and friends away from their banqueting. What kind of being, they might be asking, would disagree with such mighty mortals? It is my contention that defining "Eikon" by comparing humans to the rest of creation tells only part of the story, and not the most important. This anthropocentric and comparative approach needs to be corrected by a theocentric approach that has a fundamental missional thrust. The text of Genesis, not to mention the New Testament morphing of Genesis 1:26-27, does not *compare* Eikons to the rest of creation but instead *associates* the Eikon *with God.* The astounding element of being an Eikon is not that humans are different from animals and the land and the sky and the stars, but that they, and they alone, *are like God somehow.*

Which leads us directly to ask this question: What is God like and what does God do in Genesis 1–2 that gives us a clue to what it means to be an Eikon? God creates, God rules, God speaks, God names, God orders, God establishes variety and beauty, God makes a ducky little garden for humans, God makes a partner for Adam in Eve, God rests, and God obligates humans to himself through word and promise. Now let it be said, however, that God, in obligating his little Eikons, is not, as Dorothy Sayers said in *The Mind of the Maker,* "an old gentleman of irritable nerves who beats people for whistling."[8] God's obligations are instructions, like the ones we get in presents, for Eikons on how Eikons best work.

Now we are ready to say something about what it means to be an Eikon of God and to show its significance for shaping what the atonement is all about. To be an Eikon means, first of all, to be in union with God as Eikons; second, it means to be in communion with other Eikons; and third, it means to *participate* with God in his creating, his ruling, his speaking, his naming, his ordering, his variety and beauty, his location, his partnering, and his resting, and to oblige God in his obligating of us. Thus, an Eikon is God-oriented, self-oriented, other-oriented, and cosmos-oriented. To be an Eikon is to be a missional being—one designed to love God, self, and others and to represent God by participating in God's rule in this world. We are now back to *perichoresis*: to be an Eikon means to be summoned to participate in God's overflowing perichoretic love—both within the Trinity and in the *missio Dei* with respect to the cosmos God has created. When we participate in this *missio Dei* we become Eikonic. To be an Eikon means to be *in relationship.*

Now, what about *atonement* and the Eikon? The atonement is designed by God to restore cracked Eikons into glory-producing Eikons by participation in the perfect Eikon, Jesus Christ, who redeems the cosmos. To be an Eikon, then, is to be charged with a theocentric *and* missional life.[9] Prior to the fall, Adam and Eve did what they were supposed to do: they "eikoned." And cracked Eikons are being restored so that they can eikon now and so that they will eikon forever. As Cherith Fee Nordling puts it so well in her insightful and suggestive essay on "Being Saved as a New Creation": "I contend that to be saved is to be renewed in the true image of God as women and men in Christ, to have our relationality restored so that our sinful selves, hopelessly *incurvatus in se* [turned in on themselves], are set free to *be* new creations in true divine and human *koinōnia*."[10]

Precisely!

With Sin as Hyperrelational

Atonement theory begins also with one's view of sin. The way we define the problem shapes the way we define the solution. At times *the problem is the problem*, and probably more often than that. I randomly pulled a few books off my shelves to see how each defined "sin." I began with my friend Wayne Grudem, who in his robust Reformed manner and widely read textbook defines sin as follows: "Sin is any failure to conform to the moral law of God in act, attitude, or nature."[11] Next was the theologian J. Rodman Williams: "Sin may be defined as the personal act of turning away from God and His will. It is the transgression of God's law, yet the act is ultimately not against the law but against His person."[12] After defining sin as "first and finally" having a "Godward force," Cornelius Plantinga Jr., in what may be the best study yet on sin, *Not the Way It's Supposed to Be*, says that sin is "any agential [acts and dispositions] evil for which some person (or group of persons) is to blame. In short, sin is culpable shalom-breaking." And, "shalom is God's design for creation and redemption; sin is blamable human vandalism of these great realities and therefore an affront to their architect and builder."[13]

Plantinga is on the side of the angels: sin transcends guilt before God, sin transcends even the disposition to sin—what theologians have always called "original" sin—and sin even transcends direct sin against God. Sin is, in other words, *hyperrelational*, or "multi"-relational. It is active corruption in all directions. It is, in the oft-misused expression of Calvinism, total depravity—that is, comprehensive corruption. In the words of the Kentucky songwriter Dave Miller, who has one of the best songs on sin I've ever heard—and come to think of it, I've not heard many songs about sin—"what's wrong with me is me," and he cries out, like Peter, that "somebody needs to pull me from the raging waters I call 'me.'"[14]

Who is this "me"? The Eikon as created, Genesis tells us, was in union with God, and the Bible says this: "And it was good." That is, creation was just the way it was supposed to be. And then it becomes clear to God to Adam that "it was not good that the man should be alone" (Gen. 2:18), so God made a "helper" for him, and her name was Eve. Now Adam's relations are complete because he has an equal, someone just like him. He now has relations in four directions: Godward, selfward, otherward, and worldward.

But sin, as it is taught in the Bible, is not simply an equal distribution of these four relations: God is the One against whom humans act when they sin. Sin begins in rebellion against God and, like kudzu on southern slopes and buckthorn in northern prairies, it spreads into the other relations. Sin is the hyperrelational distortion and corruption of the Eikon's relationship with God and therefore with self, with others, and with the world. This is why theologians have always emphasized the need for humans to be first restored to God—and atonement theories that focus exclusively on sins against others fall short of a full biblical perspective on atonement, just as those that focus exclusively on God will fall short in equal measure. It won't do to get one relationship right and not the others.

The problem we face again and again in atonement theory is, in fact, the problem. We cannot discuss atonement until we define the problem that atonement remedies. If we define sin as basic mistrust (Ted Peters, Mark Biddle) that becomes pride and fear, then atonement remedies basic mistrust, pride, and fear. But these basal problems are not comprehensive enough. If sin is defined as guilt against the law, then judicial remission becomes the focus of atonement. But judicial remission, or the wiping of guilt by a declaration of justification, does not resolve the fullness of the hyperrelational problem, for it resolves only one element of the God-relation. This is why we need to see that the problem is the problem.

Thus, Wolfhart Pannenberg's point that sin is "the universal failure to achieve our human destiny," expresses our point exactly.[15] Emil Brunner says nearly the same thing: "In the Bible 'sin' does not mean something moral, but it denotes man's need of redemption, the state of the 'natural man,' seen in the light of his divine destiny."[16] Brunner's theology enables us to grasp one more element of sin as hyper*relation*ality. That is, sin in the Bible is the choice to "go it alone," to be "free" in the sense of independence, to achieve (like God) absolute freedom.[17]

But herein lies the problem: Eikons are made for union with God, communion with others, love of self, and care for the world. To strive for absolute freedom is to ask the Eikon to do what it cannot do. Eikons can't eikon alone. Eikons are made for *relationship* and to give Eikons a life without relationships, without dependence, and without love will diminish them. To pursue absolute freedom in all directions severs the Eikon from God, from others, from the world, and therefore from the self.

Severed Eikons diminish themselves.

Yet one further point about sin as hyperrelational, and it is important to atonement theory and to this book. A hyperrelational theory of sin clarifies systemic corruption. Cracked Eikons, when they coagulate into clusters, create conduits for corruption to work and they do so by creating systems that break down equity and love in various relationships. When sin is defined in such a way that it involves systemic corruption, then atonement is released to become the restoration of the Eikon in all directions, a restoration that includes the undoing of systemic corruption. Atonement, then, becomes the act of God to create a kingdom people.

These places to begin matter deeply for how atonement is understood, but we are not yet done. There are more places at which to begin.

Chapter Four

WITH ETERNITY, WITH ECCLESIAL COMMUNITY, AND WITH PRAXIS, TOO

*The old market crosses of English towns were well situated, standing where
the main streets intersected, where people met to gossip, where justice was
often done and in whose shadow went on the business of buying and selling.*
                                                                    —Paul Fiddes[1]

Theology, like an ecosystem, is an interlocking network of ideas and
beliefs and practices that meld into a coherent whole that brings into
living expression the work of God in this world. If we want to draw into a
coherent whole the Christian understanding of atonement, we will have to
begin not only with Jesus' vision of the kingdom as the macroscopic vision
of it all, but also with God as perichoresis, with Eikons, and with sin. We
will also have to have other starting points. Three more are dealt with in
this chapter.

With Eternity as Worshiping Fellowship

Our premise is simple: if eternity is like x, then life on earth ought to
be lived in tune with x. (Lived "as if.") In fact, if eternity is like x, it can be
said with utter certitude that the atonement is designed to prepare humans
for x. To be sure, we ought not to pretend, even with the highest view of
Scripture, that we know what eternity is like. At best, we get glimpses of
the Beyond and tastes of the Banquet.

Imagine being blind, which is a biblical image for humans as cracked
Eikons (Rom. 2:19; Rev. 3:17). Imagine being guided into a boat, out onto
a lake like Lake Michigan, and being given a long rod to poke the bottom.

Now describe what is at the bottom of the water. We are in the same position in seeking to describe eternity. We know some things, assuming an orthodox stance, but we can at best only try to describe the indescribable. I side with Pascal's famous wager, and in fact claim that if hope shapes identity by providing a framework for life,[2] then pondering eternity is of no small concern to all of us.[3]

There are a number of interconnecting realities about eternity in biblical visions. In Paul's vision, found in the snippet of a hymn at Philippians 2:5-11 or in the long and winding argument in 1 Corinthians 15, eternity will find all of creation and all those created *worshiping Jesus Christ* who, in turn, points to the Father so that God "may be all in all" (1 Cor. 15:28). And the Revelation has Jesus Christ, the Lamb who was slain, on the throne surrounded by myriads of worshipers—both from Israel and from the church. Around that throne four living creatures utter eternally to God: "Holy, holy, holy, the Lord God the Almighty, who was and is and is to come" (Rev. 4:8). The same worship is given also to the Lamb, who alone is worthy of such praise (5:6-10). The elders are joined by myriads of angels and then they are joined in song by "every creature in heaven and on earth and under the earth and in the sea, and all that is in them" (v. 13). A cosmic chorus of praise to God and the Son echoes down the corridors of eternity.

Alongside such visions, of course, is the obvious: humans themselves are joined in *fellowship with one another*. One is not treated to a blow-by-blow account of "who sits where" and "who gets to sit next to whom," which was the foolish question of James and John. Instead, eternity is so corporate that *individuals simply are unrecognized*, which might go a long way toward deconstructing the wooden, literal manner of those who begin to speak of ranking heavenly inhabitants. Eternity is a worshiping fellowship of God's people, and what the eternal fellowship celebrates in song is redemption and liberation—victory for the saints, defeat over Satan and Babylon, forgiveness through the blood of the Lamb, and justice and peace.

In short, eternity—wherever you look—is the same: it is a *worshiping fellowship*. This image of a worshiping fellowship symbolizes both union with God and communion with others in the context of all of creation singing out the songs of redemption. This union and communion is so pristine that it is described as a wedding feast. It will be the uninterrupted and uninterruptible communion of the covenant bond itself: "See, the home of God is among mortals. He will dwell with them as their God; they will be his peoples, and God himself will be with them" (Rev. 21:3). The Bride, it needs to be observed, is the people of God as one, here imaged in the metaphor of the New Jerusalem. That is, eternity is the *society* created by God around Jesus Christ wherein God's people enjoy union with God and communion with one another, in a place where everything works as it did in Eden.

Atonement flows from these visions. Atonement is the work of God to create and ready his people for just these things: union with God and communion with others in a place of perfection, with a society of justice and peace and above all worship of the Lamb of God on the throne.

Before we move to the next place to begin our theory of atonement, we need to observe that biblical language of eternity does not justify passivity on earth; a biblical vision of eternity stokes heated passions to yearn the way Jesus yearned—that God's kingdom might come "on earth as it is in heaven." *Any atonement theory that thinks exclusively of the earth is inadequate, just as any theory that shifts to thinking too much of eternity is also inadequate.* Nor is it wise to choose which one to emphasize; the atonement is designed for both an earthly realization and an eternal destination.

With the Ecclesial Community: Israel, Kingdom, Church

Because a central theme of *A Community Called Atonement* showcases the ecclesial focus of redemption, we will here briefly mention yet another place to begin: because God is a community of Three-in-One, God's work is always relational and community-focused. There are three words that show this, three words used so often in the Bible that they are taken for granted. The atonement benefits individuals, but always in the context of a *society* expressed with three terms in the Bible.

Israel. As soon as God got Noah and his descendants out of the ever-deepening mess they seemed to find for themselves, God formed a *covenant community.* This happens with Abraham, and the rest of the Bible—go ahead and check my facts here—is the story of Israel as a covenant community. Sometimes Israel is faithful, and sometimes not, but Israel is still God's covenant people. They have priests and a temple, they have moms and dads and kids and siblings and extended families, they have kings and subjects and military leaders and spies and scouts and enemies, they have writers and singers and poets and prophets, and they have lovers and those loved. When you look at them, they are an ordinary community with an extraordinary confidence that their God, YHWH, is the one and only God, creator and covenant-maker. A society like Israel includes individuals and yet transcends the individuals, and what amazes is that the focus of the Old Testament (or Hebrew Scriptures, the Tanakh) is on that nation as the nation with whom God established a covenant relationship.

Kingdom. Jesus decides to express his whole vision in one phrase, and he chooses "kingdom of God." It is here and it is coming, and it is small and it is big, and it is powerful and it is sometimes silent, and it is for big folks and little folks, and it is for off-the-map sinners and on-the-map righteous prigs (if they'll just learn to follow Jesus and stop thinking so highly of themselves). The kingdom, as I made clear a chapter or two back, is the society wherein God's will is established and practiced. "Kingdom," once again, is about people, about what I will call the ecclesial community.

Church. Choose your early Christian leader and you get the same emphasis: they are all for the "church" as a local expression of God's kingdom. Paul's letters are about churches—their ins and outs, the good and the bad, the things they need to learn, and the things Paul is learning about and informing them of. And he implores God to create vibrant communities of faith who will be swamped by the Holy Spirit and live like Spirit-prompted communities. And Peter says the same thing, though he talks to different people. And Hebrews, James, 1–3 John, you name it—they are all the same. God's work is with the church.

Atonement, if we read the Bible with its own emphases, is about creating communities of faith wherein God's will is done and lived out. From Genesis 12 to Revelation 22, the focus of God's redemptive work, the atoning work of God, is about the community of faith. If we don't begin here, too, we will miss what atonement is all about.

With Praxis as Reciprocal Performance

Atonement spools from the (objective) act of what God does for us into (the subjective) fresh and ongoing acts by God's people. Two words bring this emerging sense of atonement into focus: reciprocity and performance. In Kevin Vanhoozer's magnificent study of doctrine called *The Drama of Doctrine*, which builds on Hans Urs von Balthasar's *Theo-drama*, doctrine itself finds expression most emphatically *when the church performs its "script" on the world's stage.*[4] Theology, in other words, transcends proposition in *performance.* And only in its performance is theology fully in view. To claim that theology is proposition transformed into performance is not to deny the proposition; it is to say that proper theology transforms proposition into performance so that the performance is the proper proposition.

When applied to atonement, this transformation of proposition into performance becomes *reciprocity*. Two texts will make this abundantly clear. Weekly, if not daily, Christians recite a prayer that shapes atonement in a reciprocal direction. Here are the words we pray: "And forgive us our debts, as we also have forgiven our debtors." This Matthean form of the Lord's Prayer (Matt. 6:12) has a variant in the Lukan version: "And forgive us our *sins*, for we ourselves forgive everyone indebted to us" (Luke 11:4). Some have suggested that the Matthean form is closer to what Jesus actually said and that the saying speaks of economic indebtedness being overturned by the Year of Jubilee theme. That Luke's second clause has "indebted" provides support for such a view. This may be so, but there is just as strong a line of defense to argue that Matthew's use of "debts" is a metaphor for "sins," and that the Lukan "sins" is therefore justifiable. It is not my task here to adjudicate such matters, but one can easily notice that the ambiguity of the terms enables us *to see potential performative reciprocity* in the redemptive work of God.

Matthew 6:12 contends that human forgiveness and divine forgiveness are reciprocal. What term is more central to God's atoning work than "forgiveness," and which text is any clearer than this one to suggest that humans extend God's forgiveness? What could be clearer than 6:14-15, the text that trails the Lord's Prayer? "For if you forgive others their trespasses, your heavenly Father will also forgive you; but if you do not forgive others, neither will your Father forgive your trespasses." Here is a statement by Jesus that few can contest. Jesus connects our forgiveness from God and our forgiveness of others—and they are so connected that if we don't forgive others, God won't forgive us. However one wants to clarify this text, and it begs for some clarification, the connection of God's work and our work is unavoidable. The atoning God creates a community of atonement.

That very teaching is also found in the famous parable of the unmerciful servant (Matt. 18:23-35). A slave who owes a king some 10,000 talents (which is a lot of money, roughly 75 million days' wages!) begs the king for mercy, and the king magnanimously and graciously forgives the man his debts. On his ride home (I'm making this part up), that forgiven slave chances upon another slave who owes him a measly 100 denarii (which isn't a lot of money). In grand and shocking ingratitude, the forgiven slave then has the indebted slave imprisoned. Jesus doesn't find this incident amusing. His story was intended to shame us for our miserliness in reconciliation.

In fact, he asks here a piercing question, a question that finds its way into the lower shelf of every person's heart: "Should you not have had

mercy on your fellow slave, as I had mercy on you?" The king, rather jus-
tifiably we might add, tosses the previously-but-not-for-very-long-
forgiven slave into prison for life. And the point: "So my heavenly Father
will also do to every one of you, if you do not forgive your brother or sis-
ter from your heart." Here is an arresting story, informing us about the
indissoluble connection of being embraced by God's grace so that it
unleashes a cycle of humans' embracing others with grace. This is what
Brian McLaren means when he calls Jesus' kingdom message the *secret*
message of Jesus: it concerns the ongoing reconciling work of those for
whom God has shown God's own atoning work. The secret is that Jesus
establishes a community called atonement.

Forgiveness, then, is reciprocal. Which leads me to say that atonement
itself is *reciprocal* performance; it is praxis. As the follower of Jesus forgives
others their debts and sins—this is, of course, the import of the classical
statement to Peter that divides the Protestant from the Roman Catholic
(Matt. 16:19)—so the follower of Jesus is an agent of atonement. Notice
these words of the apostle Paul (2 Cor. 5:18-20):

> All this is from God, who reconciled us to himself through Christ, and has
> given us the ministry of reconciliation; that is, in Christ God was reconcil-
> ing the world to himself, not counting their trespasses against them, and
> entrusting the message of reconciliation to us. So we are ambassadors for
> Christ, since God is making his appeal through us; we entreat you on behalf
> of Christ, be reconciled to God.

God reconciles us to himself and he does this "through Christ." And then
that reconciliation is given to us so we can have a "ministry" (*ten diakon-
ian*) of "reconciliation."[5] And this is done by being an "ambassador"
(*presbuomenon*) of Christ—that is, as his personal agent of representation.
"Ambassadors" are Eikons of Christ in this world. As ambassadors, they
are extending the reconciling/atoning work of God to others. That work
involves "not counting their trespasses against them." The term "trespasses"
is the same word used in Matthew 6:14-15, and the reciprocity there and
here is similar enough to tie Paul's words to Jesus' words (at some level).
And this forgiveness is at the same time a relational reconciliation with
God: "be reconciled to God" (5:20).

To be forgiven, to be atoned for, to be reconciled—synonymous expressions—is to be granted a mission to become a reciprocal performer of the
same: to forgive, to work atonement, and to be an agent of reconciliation.
Thus, atonement is not just something done to us and for us, *it is something*

we participate in—in this world, in the here and now. It is not just something done, but something that is being done and something we do as we join God in the *missio Dei.*

Having sketched out these elements that help us begin to say what we mean by atonement, we need now to look at a more interpretive issue: the role of metaphor in discussing atonement. Which image should we use? Is there a central one? A most important one? Which image is the fairest of them all?

PART TWO

Atonement and Image: With Which Image?

C H A P T E R
F I V E

ATONEMENT AS METAPHOR: METAPHOR AND MECHANICS

Metaphor claims only an indirect purchase on reality, bringing to expression some but not all aspects and relationships of the segment of the world to which it [the metaphor] is directed.

—Colin Gunton[1]

In discussing Leo Tolstoy's theory of history, the great Russian-English émigré scholar Isaiah Berlin capitalized on a line from the Greek poet Archilochus that says, "The fox knows many things, but the hedgehog knows one big thing." Berlin contends that "Tolstoy was by nature a fox, but believed in being a hedgehog."[2] The focus of this trope is on the distinction between roaming and discovering and encountering danger over against security and familiarity and finding what has always been there.

Many theologians of the atonement are like Tolstoy: like hedgehogs, they stick with one metaphor and shape everything else in light of it or avoid anything that doesn't quite fit. Hedgehogs play a round of golf with one club. Hedgehogs are found both among the Abelardians and the Anselmians, among the incarnationists and the penal substitutionists, among the narrative *Christus Victor*-ists and the recapitulationists.[3] Foxes, unlike the hedgehogs, delight in the multiplicity of metaphors and wonder why we shouldn't explore other metaphorical gardens. They use all the clubs in their bag.

It is easy to be faithful to one biblical metaphor for the atonement—say ransom or justification—and work hard at making everything fit into that image. The difficult art of bricolage, of taking all the biblical images and combining them into an expression that manages to keep all of them in play at the same time, is much more demanding. To return to our image, we are in search of a bag in which all the clubs can fit.

Metaphors of Atonement

Atonement itself is a metaphor for everything and anything God does for us to make us what he wants to make us in light of who we were, who we are, and who we are meant to be. *Metaphor*, however, has not always been appreciated in atonement theory. Three scholars who have most helped me in this regard are Anthony Thiselton, in his magisterial *New Horizons in Hermeneutics*; Kevin Vanhoozer, in his exploration of doctrine as the performance of the script in *The Drama of Doctrine*; and especially for atonement studies, Colin Gunton in *The Actuality of Atonement*.[4] Each of these authors paves the path for a more sensitive approach to atonement through the exploration of metaphors.

Colin Gunton gets the first word: "The metaphors of atonement," he says, "are ways of expressing the significance of what had happened and was happening. They therefore enable the Christian community to speak of God as he is found in concrete personal relationship with human beings and their world." And a few pages earlier: "We must, therefore, treasure our metaphors, particularly those which have, over the centuries, commended themselves as especially illuminating in the human quest to come to terms with the meaning of our universe and of our life in it."[5]

What Is a Metaphor?

What then is a metaphor? We can begin with G. B. Caird's famous statement: "Metaphor is a lens; it is as though the speaker were saying, 'Look through this and see what I have seen, something you would never have noticed without the lens!' "[6] Or, as Sallie McFague puts it: "Most simply, a metaphor is seeing one thing *as* something else, pretending 'this' is 'that' because we do not know how to think or talk about 'this,' so we use 'that' as a way of saying something about it."[7]

Putting these two statements together and applying them toward atonement, we can say this: a metaphor of atonement is a set of lenses through which we describe *God's acts of resolving sin and of bringing humans back home in their relationship with God, with self, with others, and with the world.*

Kevin Vanhoozer sums up his theological project in a way that brings home the significance of language and metaphor. Any given theory of atonement is "not a set of timeless propositions, nor an expression of religious experience, nor grammatical rules for Christian speech and thought, but rather *an imagination* that corresponds to and continues the gospel by making good theological judgments about what to say and do in light of the reality of Jesus Christ" (emphasis added).[8] Atonement theories are imaginative metaphors that speak of the concrete reality of what God does through Jesus Christ.

Metaphor as Possibility

Metaphor is more than ornamental decoration on a more fundamental propositional reality, more than a homey story in a sermon or a clever picture to illustrate a point. Metaphors need not be stripped of their literary beauty to discover under them their propositional reality. *Au contraire*: metaphor is not a linguistic stage rehearsal but the performance itself. Anthony Thiselton claims in *New Horizons in Hermeneutics*:

> Metaphor produces *new possibilities* of imagination and vision; narrative creates *new configurations* which structure individual or corporate experience.[9]

Again, Thiselton:

> If metaphor, therefore, presents *possibility* rather than *actuality* it is arguable that metaphoric discourse can open up new understanding more readily than purely descriptive or scientific statement.[10]

The effect of seeing metaphor as *possibility* is that metaphors are not in need of decoding or unpacking but of *indwelling*. Said another way, by receiving the metaphor into the soul, the soul learns the reality. Thus, we not only indwell the metaphor, the metaphor indwells us. The charitable, loving approach to a metaphor is to let it have its way with us, and only by surrendering to it does it yield its truth.

I illustrate. As a high schooler I learned—to use a word generously—how to pole-vault for my father's track-and-field team. I learned to run down a lane as fast as I could, jam a pole into a box, and "ride" the pole into the air up and over a crossbar. Now the singular challenge (and art) of pole vaulting is learning to trust the pole with your body by keeping one arm stiff. What was so hard? When you jam that pole into the ground and hang on, the pole begins to bend. And the instant the pole begins to sag, you get this eerie sense that the pole might snap or that you are about to fall on your head onto the ground. So the temptation is to relax that arm, pull yourself up the pole, and shorten the ride (and not go as high). But if you hang on and trust the pole to do what it is designed to do—and I knew that it worked because my friend was very good at vaulting—the pole will throw you into the air and you (oh-so) "simply" guide yourself over the crossbar. (Truth be told, I managed only 10'6"; my friend vaulted about 14'.)

Some fight metaphors the way I fought the pole. And here's the downside: if you don't let metaphors do what they were designed to do, if you don't ride them out, they won't send you flying. In not trusting the metaphor to do its work, you may not collapse into a heap on the hard ground, but you'll also never know the joy of soaring with it.

For those chasing down the golf metaphor of this book, I'll put it this way: a good golfer learns to trust each club to do what each club can do. I can't ask my 7-iron to go 200 yards and I don't ask my driver to get me out of a bunker. And a good golfer learns to know her clubs so she can use the right club at the right time and let that club do what it can do.

Metaphor and the Thing

Atonement language includes several evocative metaphors: there is a sacrificial metaphor (offering), and a legal metaphor (justification), and an interpersonal metaphor (reconciliation), and a commercial metaphor (redemption), and a military metaphor (ransom). Each is designed to carry us, like the pole, to the *thing*. But the metaphor is *not* the thing. The metaphor gives the reader or hearer an *imagination* of the thing, a *vision* of the thing, a *window* onto the thing, a *lens* through which to look in order to see the thing. Metaphors take us there, but they are not the "there."

Knowing that the metaphor is not the thing leads to important implications, not the least of which is to admit in humility that we can have proper confidence in the God who atones by *indwelling* each of the many metaphors that lead us to the God who atones. We need each of them. We need justification and sacrifice and substitution and satisfaction and ransom and recapitulation and incorporation and imputation because each, in its own language game of metaphorical exploration and imagination, leads us to the core of it all: reconciliation (which is a metaphor) with God, self, others, and the world.

Perhaps most radically, we are bound to our metaphors. This is where a moderate postmodernist theology or a robust critical realist theology will simply fall down and admit that, to one degree or another, *theology is metaphorical*. We cannot unpack the metaphors to find the core, reified truth in a proposition that can be stated for all time in a particular formula. We have the metaphors and they will lead us there, but they are what we have. Yes, what we have is metaphors, but the Christian claim is that metaphors do work: they get us there.

Furthermore, as Frances Young articulates in her book *Virtuoso Theology*, not only are we bound to our metaphors, we "perform" those metaphors differently.[11] Theologians take up the metaphorical notes of Scripture and improvise, not unlike the way a good golfer can pull out a club from the bag and strike a ball surrounded by trees so that it stays below the branches and then hooks its way down a fairway and rolls up on a green.

Hans Boersma, who wrote what I think is the best theology of atonement we have to date,[12] eloquently puts all these points into a grand summary statement:

> [Metaphors] are a divinely given means to avoid idolatrous claims of knowledge. Metaphors are nonliteral descriptions of reality. They are an acknowledgment that we need to access the world around us in an indirect fashion, and that the idea of direct and complete access is an arrogant illusion that violates the multifaceted integrity of the created world.[13]

God bless you, Hans.

To understand atonement, then, is to explore metaphors that open windows onto the act of God. *How* that act of God *actually works*—its mechanics—has become a subject of intense scrutiny and can only be comprehended properly when we give way to the metaphorical nature of atonement language. Such a stance becomes most clear, perhaps, when we consider penal substitution.

Mechanics and Penal Substitution

Penal substitution contends that God is holy and that humans are sinful. God, because he is holy, can't simply ignore human sin and be true to his own holiness. So there must be a just punishment (hence, *penal*). Jesus Christ, the God-Man, stood in the sinner's place, absorbing God's just punishment on sin and sinners (hence, *substitution*). Because God demands utter perfection for entry into God's presence, not only are our sins imputed to Christ on the cross but his righteousness was then imputed to us (hence, *double imputation*). In this the mechanics are explained: God remains holy and just by judging sinners and, at the same time, forgives sin and justifies sinners by imputing Christ's obedience to us.

This theory of penal substitution has come in for hard times in current theological discussion, much of the hard times being gross caricature and political posturing. For its advocates, penal substitution is central and logically necessary for every metaphor of atonement. D. A. Carson concluded his essay on "Atonement in Romans 3:21-26" with these words:

> In short, Romans 3:25-26 makes a glorious contribution to [the] Christian understanding of the 'internal' mechanism of the atonement. It explains the need for Christ's propitiating sacrifice in terms of the just requirements of God's holy character.[14]

And Tom Schreiner contends that "the theory of penal substitution is the heart and soul of an evangelical view of the atonement."[15] For the advocates of penal substitution, this theory alone explains *how* expiation works for a holy God and sinful humans and it alone is the *logical core* of every and any orthodox theory of atonement. Not all agree. Some suggest that they are playing one club while others suggest that the club is illegal.

Critics of Penal Substitution

Joel Green and Mark Baker, in their book *Recovering the Scandal of the Cross*, contend that there are more than biblical factors at work in the attraction of some to this mechanical theory.[16] Penal substitution, they argue, fits a Western sense of justice,[17] is attractive to individualism, focuses too much on the term "wrath" in the Bible, and tends to turn the death of Jesus into something done for us rather than something to emulate.

The polemic against penal substitution has recently turned ugly. Out of the feminist movement has arisen a categorical rejection of penal substitution because of the conviction that penal substitution is violent and conveys the image of "divine child abuse"—a Father punishing the Son. Victims, so some feminists have argued, are then idealized because (1) we are taught to identify with Jesus as victim, (2) suffering is thereby justified, and (3) powerlessness is accepted. Furthermore, since the Father is good and this good God uses violence against the Son, the image of a father's violence against a child is tolerated.[18]

By taking separable elements—God's holiness, the death of Jesus, the wrath of God—and weaving them together into a rhetorical tapestry of violence and child abuse, this criticism finds a rhetorical power while it unjustly caricaturizes what is for its advocates a doctrine not of violence but of gracious identification with humans for their redemption. Penal substitution is no more inherently violent or abusive than the ransom theory is inherently triumphalist or colonizing, and no more violent than the exemplary theory is condescending. What we need most of all is to learn to treat one another's language games with respect. I appeal here to Alan Jacobs, *A Theology of Reading*, in which he radicalizes love as the only posture of hermeneutics: "Only if we understand this love of God and neighbor as the first requirement in the reading of *any* text can we fulfill 'the law of love' in our thinking, our talking, and our manner of working."[19]

Which is not to say that there isn't a language and image problem here. I was reared in penal substitution, and I saw it graphically portrayed on flannel boards as a boy and heard it exclaimed excitedly from pulpits. (It is customary to quote Jonathan Edwards' famous sermon "Sinners in the Hands of an Angry God" here.) Sometimes it was just scary to go to church, especially if some traveling evangelist had the stage. So, yes, I understand the problem. No one should question the potential for distortion and desecration. Neither do I contest the utterly sick reality that abused victims can hear the language of violence in penal substitution. But it is irresponsible for critics to depict penal substitution as "divine child abuse" because all it takes is love-of-neighbor readings of major theologians—and I will mention here Leon Morris, John Stott, and J. I. Packer[20]—and one will readily discover that for each of them penal substitution is contextualized into a Trinitarian context wherein it is not the Father being "ticked off" at humans and venting his rage on the Son. Instead, atonement for penal substitutionists is prompted by the loving grace of the Father.

But advocates of penal substitution should listen to their critics.

Nuancing Penal Substitution

Greater care should be used in articulating what is meant by penal substitution. In particular, I see two distortions and a problem present in some discussions of penal substitution. The first has to do with the "bipolarity" of God. I once heard a noted evangelical statesman say that God is bipolar in that God is both love and holy. He was using a popular expression from psychology to say something about God's dual attributes of love and holiness, but behind his words was an idea that can work theological disaster. It is the notion that God's holiness demands punishment and that his love promotes grace. Herein lies the danger of bipolarizing God, and I learned this in my first quarter of seminary from a visiting, eccentric, entertaining, hair-flapping professor: God, he gesticulated, is either loving holiness or holy love, but God is not dualistic in attributes. If one plays this dualistic language game very often, one courts the danger of turning God into a confused being who struggles over what to do with sinners.

God's wrath—and we'll leave its meaning open for now—springs as much from God's love as it does from his holiness. As Miroslav Volf puts it so well, "God isn't wrathful in spite of being love. God is wrathful *because* God is love."[21] I'd rather say that God's love is holy or that his holiness is loving than to say that God is *both* holiness *and* love if that means God's attributes are bipolarized. However we say it, and again we are brushing up against danger in using analogous language of God, we need to remind ourselves constantly to keep both in mind at all times. This is why Volf's conclusion is so resonatingly biblical: "The world is sinful. That's why God doesn't affirm it indiscriminately. God loves the world. That's why God doesn't punish it in justice."[22] What Volf summons us to is a conception of atonement that keeps both holiness and love together in God.

There is a second distortion: polarizing the persons of the Trinity. It is customary to hear critics of penal substitution contend that its advocates play one person of the Trinity over against the other: the Son steps into the gap to avert the wrath of the Father. Or the Son placates the Father on our behalf, as if God wanted to do us in and Jesus took drastic measures to get God off our case. Frankly, I had more than one friend talk like this when I was growing up. But, once again, this is another stereotype that is not true of those who have written in defense of penal substitution. And here is the point: penal substitution theories frequently contend that the Father designed and administrated the atonement plan, and if that is the case, then wrath *does not in fact change the mind of God*. Penal substitution, its advocates argue, works out the plan of the whole Trinity. But, I contend, the image conveyed can easily slip into polarizing the Father against the Son.

A third nuance must be made from the angle of rhetoric and linguistic theory and it is a criticism: by permitting themselves to describe their *theory* as "penal substitution"—when they say they believe in the "penal substitution theory" of the atonement—the advocates of this theory run the risk of playing the game of golf with one club. What I hear in those who think penal substitution is the "center" of the atonement is this: I have a bag of clubs but I like to play my 5-iron as often as possible.

That is, if this is how they talk about their theory, soon their theory will dominate which themes in the Bible they find pertinent to atonement. In particular, they will focus on wrath, on God as holy, on the cross alone (omitting life, resurrection, and Holy Spirit), and on the resolution of sin being little more than propitiation of wrath and declaration of justice— none of which I'd want to omit in a theory of atonement. A charitable reading of penal substitution theorists knows that most penal substitutionists do not reduce their theory to this, but I contend that there is a *tendency* to do so. And the way out is a more comprehensive expression for describing their "theory."

I believe the hue and cry by emerging Christians about penal substitution is a gut-level reaction to caricatures of the doctrine. I don't know how to read elements of (especially) Paul without explaining his soteriology as penal—and Howard Marshall's essay at the London School of Theology in the summer of 2005 made this (to me) abundantly clear.[23] But I am persuaded that penal substitution theorists could help us all out if they would baptize their theory into the larger redemptive grace of God more adequately. I hope to do just that in what follows, but first we need to remind ourselves of our need for humility in theology.

CHAPTER
SIX

THE MYSTERY OF OUR METAPHORS: AN EXERCISE IN POSTMODERN HUMILITY

The operative concept in postmodern theological understandings of the atonement is excess, not exchange. The death of Jesus exceeds our attempts to explain it.

—Kevin Vanhoozer[1]

A book that troubles me more about my own readings of the Bible than any I've read in my entire life is Brian Blount's *Then the Whisper Put on Flesh*. Here are some of his words that sting me deeply:

> That status of recognition belongs to the conglomeration of Euro-American scholars, ministers, and layfolk who have, over the centuries, used their economic, academic, religious, and political dominance to create the illusion that the Bible, read through their experience, *is the Bible read correctly*. [emphasis added]

And here's his stunning observation: "The whisper [of God's voice] took on a white flesh."[2] (Blount is the African American president of Union Theological Seminary.)

It is easy to contend against sociopragmatic theories of reading the Bible, as Blount's is, and claim that they are biased. *All* readings, if truth be told, are located in a theological and sociopolitical context.

How we articulate atonement is shaped by our context. The single most significant reason for carrying an entire bag of clubs is not simply because otherwise we will favor only one club, but because the club we decide to favor will be determined by our sociopragmatic concerns. Nothing makes this clearer than learning to ask questions about the central materials used to frame each club. That is, nothing makes this clearer than learning to see how we define the raw materials used to frame a doctrine of atonement. Two of the raw materials are what we mean by "human" and what we mean by "sin," and we will see that our social location shapes what we mean by both. If we learn to play all the clubs in our bag, however, we will learn to expand the meanings of both "human" and "sin."

What Is a Human?

What is a human? We are Eikons, or humans made in God's image (Gen. 1:26-27; 2 Cor. 3:18; 4:4), but we are male and female Eikons. And we are Western or Eastern, Southern or Northern, and African or African American or Asian or Asian American, and white suburban or white rural, and European or Middle Eastern or Far Eastern Eikons. And we are moms and dads, husbands and wives, neighbors and strangers, resident aliens and citizens as Eikons. We are above average or average or below average in intelligence, and we had moms who were healthy and considerate or we had moms who were unhealthy and drug addicts, even though each was an Eikon. And we had dads who were there and we had dads who weren't there, and still were Eikons. And we could go on. To answer the question "What is a human?" is not simple. And that needs to be considered as we probe the meaning of atonement for Eikons.

Does, for instance, atonement have the same meaning for an empowered suburban male as it does for an unempowered inner-city female or a rural middle-aged female? For an aristocrat as it does for an illegal immigrant? For one reared in the church—Roman Catholic, Protestant mainline/evangelical, Eastern Orthodox—or one nurtured in Islam or Hinduism or no faith or anti-faith? For one reared in the deep intoxications of capitalism or Marxism or cynicism or hatred toward all things Western? What does atonement mean for a young woman reared by loving parents who provided everything, including a good example and sound boundaries? We might speak of a common core to human nature and to atonement, but can that common core be expressed in anything other than a carefully contextualized form?

Is there such a thing as a generic common core? If not, is there such a thing as a "one-size-fits-all" theory of atonement?

What about young children who develop attachment disorders, not the least of which examples would be children neglected in overfilled and understaffed orphanages with inadequate education? What does atonement mean to such people?

Am I a soul? Am I a body? Am I both or am I, as Calvin professor of philosophy Kevin Corcoran argues, genuinely a material person who transcends the animalism and dualism of so much of our culture? We are, he says, constituted by our bodies but not identical with those bodies.[3] Corcoran seeks to find a category outside the classical materialist (I am only body) and dualist (I am body and soul, with the latter more important) views of human nature, and time will tell if he finds some consensus. What do answers to these questions say about atonement? "Much," as Paul would say, "in every way!" But do not these questions muddy the water? "Indeed!" he would come back. And all to the good, I would say, since it makes it clear that we are humans and should learn our place in this world before an infinite God who alone is fullness.

What Is Sin?

What is sin? We restrict ourselves here to the terms for sin in the Old Testament, many of which are simple metaphors. Is it rebellion (*pesha*)? Infidelity (*meshubah*)? Disloyalty (*beged*)? Getting dirty (*tum'ah*)? Wandering (*'avon*)? Trespass (*ma'al*)? Transgression (*'abar*)? Failure or missing the mark (*chatta't*)?

And now we can expand these terms to various understandings of how to put them all together. Is sin—as I think it is—distortion in all directions, toward God, self, others, and the world? Is sin systemic injustice and systemic distortion? How do we define sin? What is its essence? Is it pride, is it selfishness, is it fear, is it the hubris of Prometheus or the spinelessness of the traitor or the treachery and barbarity of the Nazis?

The problem for atonement is the problem (sin) it resolves—that problem (sin) is itself a problem.

Sin is complex. Some deny its existence as an objective entity, while others shove it entirely into the realm of the systemic but give it a real existence—whether political, economic, or ideological. Some focus on personal responsibility and the loss of sin in our culture. The deeper we get into sin the more complex it becomes. The more we probe into the meaning of sin the more we come to what theologian Ted Peters observes: "Perhaps the only way to get at the truth of sin is through confession."[4] And a good place to begin confession is Isaiah 59 (and you should read the whole chapter):

For our transgressions before you are many,
    and our sins testify against us.
Our transgressions indeed are with us,
    and we know our iniquities:
transgressing, and denying the LORD,
    and turning away from following our God,
talking oppression and revolt,
    conceiving lying words and uttering them from the heart.
Justice is turned back,
    and righteousness stands at a distance;
for truth stumbles in the public square,
    and uprightness cannot enter.
Truth is lacking,
    and whoever turns from evil is despoiled. (59:12-15)

Questions abound. Is sin the same for a male as it is for a female? Some think this question is like kicking straight into the pointed goads while others sees this as turning sin loose on life's real roads. Is the recent claim that males define sin in male-ish ways as pride and power justifiable? Does this definition mean that the powerless (including females) are kept in their powerlessness because the powerful have defined sin in light of their own problems? Whether or not one wants to radicalize this suggestion, the point has merit. Is sin the same for an African American as it is for a South African as it is for a Kenyan? For Europeans as it is for Asians? For Israelis as it is for Palestinians?

Can we get behind each of these particulars to discover the essence of sin? Mark Biddle, in his exceptional, thoroughly biblical study on sin, *Missing the Mark*, concludes that sin's essence is *basic mistrust* that manifests itself as pride and fear—as seeking to be both more than we are and less than we are. Ted Peters sees sin as the "human attempt to fixate the present and resist God's future—that is, to absolutize our own part and sacrifice God's whole."[5] Here again we have mistrust shaped by hubris.

Isn't sin bigger than its essence? Again, the answer is yes. Sin is not only that "act" of basic mistrust that finds its way into peccadillo and pride, but also a human condition of sinfulness and systemic corruption. Sin takes on a life of its own, like kudzu and buckthorn, and it takes more than a little effort to rid the hillsides of both of those infestations. Sin is, Plantinga says, "both fatal and fertile."[6]

I believe the problem atonement resolves is sin, but that problem (sin) is itself a problem because we can't grasp its massive dimensions.

Plantinga's combination of the words "fertile and fatal" strikes me. Is sin fertile in fatality or fatal in its fertility? Probably both. In what sense is sin fatal? Augustine, that towering theologian of Hippo, addresses this issue. He contends that good things can be corrupted, which leads him to this arresting conclusion: "I sought to know what wickedness was, and found *it was no substance*, but a perverse distortion of the will away from the highest substance and towards the lowest things" (*Confessions* 7.16.22, emphasis added; see also *City of God* 11.22; 19.13).[7] Which is to say that evil does not exist, but is only the diminution and distortion and perversion and corruption of the good. Or, again, as Plantinga puts it, "the person who curves in on himself . . . ends up sagging and contracting into a little wad."[8] Do we say that sin "is" or do we say that sin really is nothing more than diminution of God's good things?

As if these concerns don't create enough complexity in the metaphors for sin, there is more. In his recent study dealing with how atonement strikes home for postmoderns, British theologian Alan Mann contends that postmoderns live in a "sinless" society.[9] Now Mann does not deny the reality of sin, nor does he believe that postmoderns are somehow innocent. Instead, he is contending that postmoderns tend to be *pre*moral rather than *a*moral. Which means that defining sin as offending God (the Ultimate Other) does not strike home because not only is the postmodern premoral, he and she are also adrift from others—making the notion of an offense against Someone or someone doubly difficult for them.

I don't know that many will agree with Mann (and others like him), but let us at least admit to this: there are real differences in the big epochs in history when it comes to perceptions of sin. Once we admit that sin defines how we approach atonement, we are driven to the conclusion that atonement is a challenge because of the mind-numbing complexity of sin.

Humans whose sin problem is resolved by the atoning work of Christ may only over time realize the depth of what that original problem really was. As I say, the problem more often than not is the problem. Perhaps Ted Peters has this right: we only know sin by confession. Does that mean, then, that we only know atonement by faith and grace?

What, Then, Is Atonement?

Theologians, both in the Bible and after the Bible, have come up with five big metaphors for atonement: incorporation (into Christ, who recapitulated Adam's life), ransom or liberation, satisfaction, moral influence, and penal substitution. Which shall we choose? Do we need to choose? Yes we do. At each spot on the course we have to take a club from the bag and use it.

Again, if you begin with humans as generic Eikons, you get atonement at the generic level. But if you begin with a Mexican American female immigrant and if you speak of sin as the fear of trusting God in order to become what God made her to be in Christ, you just might discover that atonement is liberation from oppression that is accomplished by being incorporated into Christ and empowered by the Spirit and connected to the fellowship of a local church.

Our central question here has been asked by theologian Vincent Bacote: "How is salvation understood from the perspective of communities with significant legacies of oppression and victimization?"[10] What about those who have, as he puts it, "lumps in their spirits"? What does atonement mean for the young girl who grew up in a good home with good parents and good siblings and good friends, but who somehow wanders away from all that goodness? Who, after a decade or so of wandering and a failed marriage and now a kid perched on each hip, returns home and discovers that a life lived outside the good graces of God and love brings intense guilt and wants forgiveness? What does atonement mean for her? Which theory of atonement will work for her?

Another example: What does atonement mean for a white male suburban kid whose parents are wealthy, whose needs have been met, whose path is straight and flat and heading right back to the suburbs, where he will create a suburban cycle of comfort? Some may wish to disparage the suburban kid and encourage the Mexican American female immigrant—when we ought to be arguing that sin is complex enough and the atonement big enough that each person needs encouragement to find atonement in Jesus Christ. Again from Bacote, addressing his fellow evangelicals: "If we have focused on only half of the gospel, half of the truth, then do we have the truth at all?"[11] Salvation, and therefore atonement's intent, Bacote answers, is public, political, pneumatological, and concerned with a particular place.

If this chapter does anything for us, I hope it magnifies God by showing who we really are, by multiplying sin and by enlarging our sense of atonement. Our grasp of atonement is partial; the God we are grasping for is complete and whole. In God there is absolute truth; in our articulations there is always something lacking, something partial, and something still yearning for yet more. A proper confidence in the God who atones reminds us of this and keeps us humble—and in conversation as we work this atonement thing out in each generation.

Questions about human nature, sin, and atonement are intertwined, forcing us at times to mix our metaphors, leading us yet further into the deeper mysteries of what atonement is all about.

In our search to find an expression that expresses what atonement is all about, not only do we recognize the value of metaphor, but we must also deal with the crucial "atoning moments" in God's action on our behalf. To do this, we need to examine each moment separately to lead us to an expression that brings them all together.

CHAPTER
SEVEN

ATONING MOMENTS:
CRUX SOLA?

In Christ as sacrifice, God our judge is judged in our place, reveals our per-
petration of and collaboration with sin, ends our rebellion, forgives our guilt,
cleanses us, makes us righteous, and establishes us in the kingdom of peace.
—Jonathan Wilson[1]

To speak of atonement is to find oneself in a story. Atonement
metaphors create a story with a *beginning* (created as Eikons) and an
end (glorifying, fellowshipping Eikons), and they also put into that story a
conflict (cracked Eikons as individuals and as groups) and a *resolution*
(Eikons healed in all four directions: God, self, others, world). In particular, atonement metaphors—like reconciliation—especially focus on the
impact of the things God has done in history to resolve the conflict in the
biblical story. To latch onto an expression that brings all of this together
into a single bag, we must first examine the "moments of atonement"
when God acted to redeem creation and resolve the conflict.

The cross is the center of the atonement. Of course, there would be no
cross were it not for God becoming human (the incarnation). And without
the resurrection, the cross's work would be incomplete. But neither of those
points can be permitted to minimize how important the death of Jesus is to
the New Testament authors and to theologians like Luther. So we need
briefly to remind ourselves of the centrality of the cross for atonement.

Paul

The apostle Paul said this: "we proclaim Christ crucified" (1 Cor. 1:23).
Just as Jesus could summarize Torah as loving God and loving others
(Mark 12:28-31), so Paul could summarize God's redemptive work as the

cross. Until we see the genius of Paul's summarization, we cannot comprehend the atonement.

Paul ransacked his own vocabulary to describe what God did through Christ. He chose a word from the commercial or military world—redemption; one from the cultic world—mercy seat or "sacrifice of atonement" (Rom. 3:25); one from the covenant and law world—justification; and one from the relational world—reconciliation. The metaphors Paul chose determined the problem they addressed: if the word is redemption, the problem is slavery; if the word is sacrifice of atonement, the problem is sin or falling short of God's glory; if the word is reconciliation, the problem is alienation. However, if the result determines the problem because it is inherent to the metaphor, the *means of resolution* each time is the same. Eikons are liberated, sacrificed for, justified, and reconciled to God, self, others, and the world by one and the same act: the death of Jesus Christ. Thus, from Romans 3:21-25 we see that redemption, our liberation, and the sacrifice of atonement are found in the "blood" of Jesus Christ—an image of his death. Paul can say we are "justified by his blood" (5:9) but also that we are "reconciled to God through the death of his Son" (5:10-11).

The central act of atonement is the cross. More of this in chapter 9 below.

Martin Luther and the Cross

No single theologian ever spoke more emphatically of the cross than Martin Luther. One might say that the cross became the lens through which Luther saw all of theology. No, strike that: he *did* see all of theology through the lens of the cross.

On October 31, 1517, Martin Luther pinned his famous Ninety-Five Theses upon Indulgences (indulgences funded St. Peter's in Rome) to the door of the church in Wittenberg, challenging the church to mend its ways. When summoned to defend himself on April 26, 1518, Luther held forth in what is called the *Heidelberg Disputation*. Here, at the very beginning of his illustrious career as a reformer, Luther set down for all to hear and read the foundations of what it means to be a theologian of the cross in bold contrast to a theologian of glory.[2] In this disputation Luther established a famous *sola*, adding to the already-established reforming principles of *sola scriptura, sola gratia, and sola fide*—"Scripture alone, by grace alone, and through faith alone." Luther's new *sola* was this: *crux sola est nostra theologia*—"the *cross alone* is our theology."

What is a *crux sola*—a cross-alone—theology? Luther, we must remember, is being called to account and his response is to offer a theology radically infiltrated by the cross itself. His thesis is that there are two kinds of theologians: theologians of the cross and theologians of glory. A theologian of *glory* claims to see into the invisible things of God by peering *through* earthly things—events, works, and so on (thesis 19). Hence, what we might call a "natural" theologian. A theologian of the *cross*, however, "comprehends the visible and manifest things of God seen through suffering and the cross" (thesis 20).

However we look at Luther today, the point needs to be made with regular emphasis: Luther summoned not just theologians but *theology itself* to the cross. Without a theology of the cross, the atonement dissipates. The question is this: Does atonement encompass more than the cross? The rhetoric of Luther could lead some to think that Luther thought everything occurred on Good Friday, but his other writings demonstrate that although he believed that the cross was the necessary gate into the community called atonement, other moments were also involved in God's gracious work for us. Have others been as comprehensive as Luther? I'm afraid not. For some the cross remains a crucifix. For Luther the cross was empty. The difference between a *crux sola* theology of the crucifix and a *crux sola* theology involving all the moments of atonement is enormous.

In what follows, I will suggest that atonement is a *crux et*—the cross and . . . the resurrection and Pentecost, each set into the incarnation and the manifestation of God in the ecclesial community. We need to begin this absorption of the cross into the redemptive moments by pausing to look at the significance of something we've already briefly touched upon: the incarnation.

C H A P T E R
E I G H T

ATONING MOMENTS:
INCARNATION AS SECOND
ADAM

But following the only true and stedfast Teacher, the Word of God, our Lord
Jesus Christ, who did, through His transcendent love, become what we are,
that He might bring us to be even what He is Himself.

—Irenaeus[1]

The rise of Jesus studies in the last three decades creates an opportunity
to develop the significance of Jesus' own life in God's redemptive plan.
If a *crux sola* theology has the tendency at times to neglect that life to contend
that Jesus came (only) to die, the kind of theology emerging today flows from
the Trinitarian *perichoresis* directly into the moment of the incarnation itself,
the day Mary said, "Let it be with me according to your word" (Luke 1:38).

The atoning significance of the incarnation is expressed both by
Irenaeus and Athanasius: "God became what we are so that we might
become what He is." The implication of this observation shapes the
entirety of what we mean by the atonement: God *identifies* with us in the
incarnation. Without identification, without incarnation, there is no
atonement. Which is to say that the atonement is an ontological act—
God's sharing our nature and our sharing God's—at its core: it is about
God *identifying* with us so that we might participate in God (2 Pet. 1:4).

Incarnation as Identification with Us

We begin with Matthew 1:18-25. Joseph, a *tsadiq* ("observant"), receives
a revelation from an angel informing him that he will be husband to Mary
and "father" to a son. This son, however, will be conceived virginally and

will bring *salvation* to Israel (1:21; hence the name Jesus from Yeshu'a ["YHWH saves"]). All of this fulfills the (interpreted) prophecy of Isaiah 7:14: " 'Look, the virgin shall conceive and bear a son, and they shall name him Emmanuel,' which means, 'God is with us' " (Matt. 1:23). This Christmas text can become too familiar for us to see what it is saying. Matthew connects three themes here: the virginal conception, salvation, and God "with us." Incarnation means *identification* for the sake of liberation.

Another text to consider is John 1, in which John describes what God has done in the incarnation as he converses with Genesis 1:1-2 and Proverbs 8:22-31.[2] Thus:

> In the beginning when God created the heavens and the earth, the earth was a formless void and darkness covered the face of the deep, while a wind from God swept over the face of the waters. (Gen. 1:1-2)

> The LORD created me at the beginning of his work,
>   the first of his acts of long ago.
> Ages ago I was set up,
>   at the first, before the beginning of the earth.
> When there were no depths I was brought forth,
>   when there were no springs abounding with water.
> Before the mountains had been shaped,
>   before the hills, I was brought forth—
> when he had not yet made earth and fields,
>   or the world's first bits of soil.
> When he established the heavens, I was there,
>   when he drew a circle on the face of the deep,
> when he made firm the skies above,
>   when he established the fountains of the deep,
> when he assigned to the sea its limit,
>   so that the waters might not transgress his command,
> when he marked out the foundations of the earth,
>   then I was beside him, like a master worker;
> and I was daily his delight,
>   rejoicing before him always,
> rejoicing in his inhabited world
>   and delighting in the human race. (Prov. 8:22-31)

The astounding claims of John's Gospel are these: *first*, that the Creator of Genesis 1:1-2 is the *Logos*; *second*, that the One who is Wisdom in Proverbs 8, who entered the world but could not find a receptive home, is this *Logos* and this *Logos* has found a home among Jesus' followers; *third*, and more remarkable than these two connections, is that this *Logos* has become flesh. What separates Christianity from Judaism, as Daniel Boyarin so ably notes, is not *Logos* theology *per se*, but the belief that the *Logos* is Jesus.[3] It is all about God becoming one of us.

Observe that John is not a speculative or theoretical theologian. Incarnation is about the flow of life from God to us. Observe the missional shape of the incarnation. First, since the *Logos* is Creator and becomes human, the Crea*tor* becomes like the crea*ted* to give new life to creation. Second, the true *light* enters into *darkness* in order to send darkness marching back home. This true light gives (new) birth to those who "receive" the *Logos* by simply trusting him as that true light. Third, a new birth becomes available from God and this new birth grants eternal life. Fourth, the *Logos* becomes "enfleshed" (1:14) and that "enfleshment" is perceived by those born from above as the very revelation of God's glory so that all receive "grace upon grace" out of his "fullness" (1:16). In each turn of phrase, the incarnation is about identifying with humans in order to bring them to God—creation, light, life, and grace.

Here's the significance: the incarnation, which sums up the entirety of Jesus' earthly existence (not just his birth), is an atoning moment. In the incarnation, God identifies with humans—all humans in all the dimensions of human life—to bring humans grace. He becomes what we are so we can become what he is.

The Temptations of Jesus

The temptation narrative about Jesus is also about the incarnation. Very few texts have been more misused than the story of Jesus being tempted to make bread, to jump off of the temple, and to seize control of the kingdoms of this world (Matt. 4:1-11 and Luke 4:1-13). Many Christians read this text and think that we learn from Jesus how to encounter temptation. That is, when tempted, we should quote Bible verses and Satan will be sure to fly away to some cave. There is not a word of this in the text; it says nothing directly about how to endure temptation. Theologians have long contemplated this text and have seen two major themes, and both of them—one more profoundly than the other—get to the heart of Jesus' encounter with the Enemy.

Some think Jesus relives in the temptation experience the original experience of Adam and Eve in Eden. That is, Jesus' experience in the wilderness is a *second Eden* experience, with Jesus being a *second Adam (and Eve)*.

But unlike Adam and Eve, Jesus does not fall into sin. This second Adam (and Eve) understanding is sometimes preferred by scholars, but the majority today prefer to see in Jesus' temptations a *second wilderness experience.* Jesus is being tempted as Israel was tempted in the wilderness wanderings. Again, Jesus goes through the wilderness without falling to the temptations of the flesh and pride and provocation. In both interpretations, Jesus *becomes one of us* (the essence of incarnation) and undergoes what others went through as Adamites or Evites or the wandering Israelites.

How to decide between the two? This one, so I think, is easy: the Gospel texts overtly connect Jesus' experience to Deuteronomy *and Israel's wilderness experience* and not to Adam and Eve's experience in Eden. When tempted to make bread, Jesus quotes from Deuteronomy 8:3; when tempted to jump off of the temple, Jesus quotes Deuteronomy 6:16; and when tempted to seize the kingdoms, Jesus quotes Deuteronomy 6:13. *Each of these texts is from Israel's wilderness experience.* Clearly, then, Jesus is being depicted as a second Israel and his experience is in a second wilderness. He rolls back history *to become what Israel was* so he can undo what Israel did.

This text has nothing to do with Jesus being an example for dealing with temptations. We are not—at least I hope we are not—tempted to fast for forty days and then turn stones into plump, fragrant little loaves of bread; we are not tempted to jump from the temple (or tall buildings) to show others how God will protect us from harm; and we are not tempted to come into possession of all the kingdoms of this world. And if we are, we are probably on the order of a megalomaniac, in which case I suppose such a person would not be reading this book about atonement. Not only are these temptations not ours, there is nothing in this text that suggests we are to take strength in learning from Jesus how to attack temptations by quoting Scriptures—though one would hardly recommend a better strategy (other than not fasting too long, not jumping off buildings, etc.). In fact, I'm quite prepared to suggest that it is tantamount to the preposterous to suggest that Jesus is being an example here.

The temptations of Jesus are not exemplary for us so much as they are about the incarnation. Jesus is qualified to be the savior and leader of the new Israel by being the perfect Israelite in the same old wilderness of temptation. The emphasis of the temptation narrative is clearly not on the *result* of the temptations, but instead on the contrast between Israel in the wilderness and Jesus in the wilderness. The emphasis is on a new people being created "in" Jesus because he encounters the wilderness and comes out victorious.

Incarnation is also found in other themes in which a connection to atonement is made.

Perfect Eikon

The apostle Paul liked assigning to Jesus the vocation that was assigned to Adam and Eve in Genesis 1:26-27: as Adam and Eve were created to be *Eikons*, so Jesus Christ is the Creator and *Eikon*. In fact, we can reverse this order and get to the bottom of what Paul is saying: because Jesus is the perfect Eikon, God made Adam and Eve as Eikons to reflect the perfect Eikon.

Paul can speak of Jesus Christ as "the *Eikon* of God" (2 Cor. 4:4), and he can say that God's cosmic, redemptive (atoning) intent is that humans might be "conformed to the *Eikon* of his Son" (Rom. 8:29). And, just as we have borne the "*Eikon* of the man of dust" (Adam), so we will bear the "*Eikon* of the man of heaven" (Christ; 1 Cor. 15:49). In fact, God's redemptive plan involves transforming his people "from one degree of [*Eikonic*] glory to another" (2 Cor. 3:18) through the Spirit. What this Eikon theology shows is that Jesus was the perfect human being: he completely identified with humans. And this identification was designed with redemptive intent.

Second Adam

Romans 5:12-21 speaks of the significance of the incarnation for redemption with another term, this time "Adam": Jesus is the *second Adam*. That is, *what Adam did, Jesus undid to excess.* Adam disobeyed God and brought death, but Jesus obeyed God and so passed on (abundant, eternal) life for all. Adam's singular act passes on judgment, but Jesus' singular act establishes (abundant) righteousness for all. The following displays Paul's theology of the second Adam:

Paul begins with Adam as Eikon:

Adam is Eikon. But Adam sins.
Sin enters the world through Adam.
Sin brings death to the Eikon.

Paul connects Jesus to Adam as the second Adam:

Jesus is the second Adam and Eikon.
But Jesus lives obediently.

Jesus' identification brings redemption:

Grace/gift abounds: the life of Jesus turns back death and gives life.
Fallen Adamites are justified.
Reborn Adamites are given eternal life.

The life Jesus lives in his time on earth, a life summed up as "one man's act of righteousness," somehow stops the death flow from Adam. However, not only does his act of righteousness absorb and erase the debt of Adam, it actually creates a life flow for those in Christ. While some might narrow this one act of righteousness to the choice on Jesus' part to die on the cross, Paul's intent seems to be more comprehensive than that: it is Jesus himself, *the one whose entire life (including the cross) was an act of obedience*, who brings life. Again, atonement flows from incarnational identification and involves the life of Jesus as well as his death (and resurrection).

What ought to be emphasized here is that Jesus is the second Adam, not the second Abraham. To be the second Adam means Jesus has brought redemption for the entirety of Adam's line—for all humans. Adam and his line are given a brand new start, a new creation, "in Christ."

Union with Christ as Identification with Christ

To say that Jesus is the second Adam ushers us directly to the importance of *union with Christ*. If "in" Adam we sin and die, so "in" Christ we become righteous and live. In other words, it is all about "with and to whom" we are united. Jesus is the second Adam who, through the whole of his incarnation, incorporates us into *his* life. The upshot of this is enormous: *everything that is Christ's becomes ours by being united to him*. Everything, including wisdom and righteousness and sanctification and redemption, comes to us because we are united to the incarnate one (1 Cor. 1:30).

Emphasizing union with Christ foregrounds a relational theory of the atonement. My own reading of the Reformed thinkers on atonement leads me to contend that many of them deemphasize the relational aspects because they deemphasize "union with Christ" and Christ as second Adam. A Reformed thinker who gets this right is D. A. Carson: "I cannot too strongly emphasize how often Paul's justification language is tied to 'in Christ' or 'in him' language…" and "justification is, in Paul, irrefragably tied to our incorporation into Christ, to our union with Christ." He also comments, "Some think of imputation and union with Christ in frankly antithetical terms, instead of seeing the *latter* [i.e., union with Christ] *as the grounding of the former* [i.e., imputation]" (emphasis added).[4] Perhaps a citation from John Calvin will seal the deal:

> Therefore, that joining together of Head and members, that indwelling of Christ in our hearts—in short, that mystical union—are accorded by us the highest degree of importance, so that Christ, having been made ours, makes us sharers with him in the gifts with which he has been endowed. We do not, therefore, contemplate him outside ourselves from afar in order that his righteousness may be imputed to us *but because we put on Christ and are engrafted into his body—in short, because he deigns to make us one with him.*[5] (emphasis added)

And Calvin then calls our righteousness a "fellowship of righteousness with him."

Now briefly, Philippians 2:5-11, because here again we find incarnation connected to redemption. The context of this beautiful hymn is one of learning to live the life of Christ as a community, and that will mean "mimicking" the *perichoresis* of God revealed in the incarnation of Christ Jesus. This Christ Jesus was in the very "form of God" but surrendered that "equality" so that he could rescue cracked Eikons from their condition and lead them into the glorious presence of God. How so? *By identifying with humans* even to the point of death on the cross. Here Jesus is depicted as both a second Adam and a second Israel who, through an entire life of surrendering service for others, was raised to the right hand of God.

This hymn (Phil. 2:5-11) may well be the most complete statement of the atoning work that we can find in the entire New Testament. Again, the entire life of Jesus—birth, loving service, humiliating death, resurrection, and ascension—atones for cracked Eikons so that they might be led to the very presence of God in eternity. Until that time, Eikons are to live out the life God is working in them by living as Christ lived (2:13).

A *crux sola* theory of atonement is inadequate, but not because there is something insufficient in the cross. The atonement begins in the *perichoresis* of God, that eternal communion of interpersonal love, and that *perichoresis* becomes incarnate in the Son of God, the *Logos*, Christ Jesus, who assumes—hence the cross—what we are (cracked Eikons) in order to draw us into that *perichoresis*. And it is the entire life of Jesus (not to mention yet Pentecost) that creates atonement. A genuinely biblical atonement is incarnational as it sets the stage now for what happens in the cross.

Chapter Nine

ATONING MOMENTS: CRUCIFIXION

There is then, it is safe to say, no Christianity without the cross. If the cross is not central to our religion, ours is not the religion of Jesus.
—John R. W. Stott[1]

I agree with Martin Luther: we need a theology shaped by the cross. I agree with John Stott: there is no Christianity without the cross. I agree with Jürgen Moltmann: "At the centre of Christian faith is the history of Christ. At the centre of the history of Christ is his passion and his death on the cross."[2]

The only table of fellowship in the Christian faith is the wooden table that morphs into a wooden cross. When a theory of atonement contends that the cross is not central to the plan of the atoning God, that theory dissolves the only story the church has ever known.

This book is dedicated to deconstructing one-sided theories of the atonement. It is also dedicated to demonstrating that the cross is inseparable from the incarnation and resurrection of Jesus, Pentecost, and the ecclesial focus of the work of God. And this book is dedicated to deconstructing simplistic, individualistic theories of the atonement. The atonement—from beginning to end—is designed to resolve the macroscopic problem of evil and sin generated by Adam and Eve in Eden. The massive dimensions of sin—distortion in four directions: with God, self, others, world—are met by the massive resolution of sin in Jesus Christ, centered as it is in the cross.

And the cross, set in that context, is the work of God to restore cracked Eikons to union with God and communion with others for a missional life focused on others and the world.

Mark and the Cross: Evil in a Moment

To understand the cross in biblical context requires a full-orbed perception of God's redemptive design, which means a full-orbed comprehension of humans as Eikons and what sin is and what sin does to humans and the world. In other words, the cross addresses not only *my* problem as sinner but *our* problem as sinners gathered together in what is best called systemic injustice and evil. Which means that the cross addresses *the problem of evil*. We are not being fair to the Pauline texts on the cross if we narrow them simply and woodenly to resolution of *my* sin problem. The cross addresses *our* sin problem—"our" in the sense of yours and mine and the Western world's and the Eastern world's and the northern and southern hemispheres' problems. It addresses *the world's captivity by evil*.

This book is not big enough to deal with all of this, so I wish here to discuss briefly how Mark tells the story of the cross. Sin for Mark finds expression in three nodes. First, there is a *cosmological and spiritual* revolt against the presence of Jesus, the Son of Man, in history. Jesus enters the wilderness and is "tempted by Satan" (Mark 1:13); he enters the synagogue and a man with an unclean spirit cries out, "What have you to do with us, Jesus of Nazareth? Have you come to destroy us? I know who you are, the Holy One of God" (1:23-24). And Jesus declares that his own mission is to bind up the strong man (the prince of demons): "No one can enter a strong man's house [the world] and plunder his property [victory over evil] without first tying up the strong man [defeating Satan]" (3:27).

Second, there is a *human* revolt against the presence of Jesus. Mark 2 and 3 detail the opposition Jesus' countercultural, boundary-breaking ministry created: scribes, the disciples of John, Pharisees, and others, one after the other—as if we are watching a staged play—appear on the scene to offer their criticisms of Jesus. The summary conclusion is found in Mark 3:6: "The Pharisees went out and immediately conspired with the Herodians against him [so they might find a way to] destroy him." Third, there is a *political* revolt against the presence of Jesus, whose mission it was to destroy evil, forgive sin, and establish justice. Jesus enters Jerusalem that last week to provoke response: he is questioned about his authority, about Caesar's rule and role, about the resurrection, and about the greatest commandment (Mark 11:1–12:34). Finally, Jesus counters with a question of his own: Whose son is the Messiah (12:35-37)? Then Jesus predicts the demise of Jerusalem because its leaders cooperate with sin, evil, and injustice (chap. 13). The authorities—both Jewish and especially Roman—put

Jesus on trial and find him guilty of sedition, leading to his crucifixion (14–15).

Now we can understand the cross from Mark's perspective: it is the convergence of evil against the presence of God's saving work to end injustice and sin and to create justice and holiness. The evil machinations of all are heaped upon Jesus.

The paradox is clear: what is understood to be the ending of a powerful threat becomes the creation of a new day, a new order, and a new redemption. This is hinted at in Jesus' regular victories over the cosmological and spiritual forces through exorcisms (1:25-26, 32-34; 3:11-12) and in his stunning victories after public accusations (2:1–3:6). Jesus goes down according to the designs of evil but he comes back up the victor over the arrogant injustices of unjust rulers. He is not only announced as the Son of God by a Roman centurion at the ultimate moment of injustice (15:39)—Luke's parallel has "just man" (Luke 23:47)—but he is also raised from the dead, just as he predicted (Mark 16:1-8; cf. 8:31).

Sin and evil do not get the last word. The last word is the cross, the empty cross, the cross that liberates humans from themselves and from sin and that liberates them for God, self, others, and the world.

Let me put this together: in Mark's Gospel the cross is simultaneously the sick display of injustice and the magic of new creation, both a hideous demonstration of evil and the glorious moment of love. Jesus enters into the world of cracked Eikons who have, each in their own way, worked against God's resolution, and broken the powers of this world through the cross and resurrection.

The cross in Mark is about evil from all the corners of the globe and the human heart converging in one moment and on one person: Jesus of Nazareth. Jesus not only dies for us, he dies "with us." He identifies with us all the way down to death on a cross. The cross, then, is not just a solitary act of one man, Jesus Christ, to redeem solitary individuals, you and me. Instead, it stands as a cosmological, spiritual, and political act of evil into which God enters to identify with humans in order to turn the cosmological, spiritual, and political powers on their head. The cross creates the kingdom as Jesus envisions it.

Paul and the Cross

Only with this in mind can we approach the single most important text in Pauline soteriology: Romans 3:21-26. The first thing to be said is that

Paul's "Christ crucified" message is a Christ-still-on-the-cross message. That is why, in the poetic words of T. S. Eliot, we say, "Again, in spite of that, we call this Friday good."[3] Why is it good? Because the real cross with Christ on it became, three days later, a real cross with Christ no longer on it. We can explore why that Good Friday is good by looking at a singular text in Romans 3, a text riddled with theological controversy but still standing as the most significant atonement passage in the New Testament. If traditionalists have ignored the theme of the kingdom of God in constructing an atonement theory, some contemporary reshapings have ignored passages like Romans 3:21-26—a passage preeminently concerned with the cross. Because the cross figures in most of what follows, I will simply sample this one text as we move onward in our construction of a bag big enough to hold all of the atonement clubs.

Romans 3:21-26

> But now, apart from law, the righteousness of God has been disclosed, and is attested by the law and the prophets, the righteousness of God through faith in Jesus Christ for all who believe. For there is no distinction, since all have sinned and fall short of the glory of God; they are now justified by his grace as a gift, through the redemption that is in Christ Jesus, whom God put forward as a sacrifice of atonement by his blood, effective through faith. He did this to show his righteousness, because in his divine forbearance he had passed over the sins previously committed; it was to prove at the present time that he himself is righteous and that he justifies the one who has faith in Jesus.

To preface our discussion, we have to factor in one significant element: the cross is the climactic vortex of the incarnation (as Phil. 2:5-11 states). Jesus' death is not a one-off event, but the penultimate event—resurrection comes next—of his entire incarnate life. So, whatever is said about the cross, it begins with this: on the cross Jesus *identifies with us in our suffering, in our pain, and in our death.*

I can only offer brief comments on Romans 3:21-26, and my intent is to show that Paul sees God's act on the cross to be one in which cracked Eikons are healed by forgiveness.[4] *First*, humans are sinners because "all have sinned," and in light of 5:12-21 we can conclude that this "sin" is done both in Adam and in actual practice by each person. This is the point of 1:18–3:20, after all.

Second, God's "right-making" (or "righteousness" or "justifying work" or "making the world right" or "declaring people right")—notice the pre-eminence of "right-making" as God's act—comes to pass according to the Torah but not by obeying the Torah. This right-making (justification) is God's saving action to make humans right and to put the world to rights.[5]

Third, God's "right-making" occurs in and through "faith in/of Jesus Christ." Here we meet up with a contemporary problem: Does "faith of Jesus Christ" mean faith *in* Jesus Christ (Christians trust Christ) or the faith *of* Jesus Christ *himself* (Christ faithfully lives before God)? One might be tempted to agree with Origen: the language is sufficiently ambiguous to permit both ideas at once.[6] To the degree that Jesus is the second Adam/Israel who identifies with us in his incarnation, it is *his* faithfulness to the covenant; to the degree that Jesus is our (alien) righteousness (1 Cor. 1:30-31), it is *our* faith in Jesus Christ. However, that Paul continues on with "for all who believe" leads me to agree with Jimmy Dunn that what Paul has in mind is the disposition of believers: they trust in Christ for their right-making.[7]

Fourth, this right-making by God is for everyone, both Jew and Gentile (and not just for Jews).

Fifth, back to a previous point: God's right-making is a gracious act on the part of God. The atoning work of God flows freely from the divine *perichoresis* of mutual, interpenetrating love and grace that inevitably flows through Christ into the cracks of cracked Eikons.

Sixth, the grace of God for cracked Eikons finds verbal expression in three metaphors, each of which plays its own language game and each of which overlaps with the others: God "declares/makes right" (justification) and "redeems" (redemption), and God does this on the "mercy seat." Some translations have "sacrifice of atonement," others "propitiation," and yet others "expiation." The Greek term (*hilasterion*) refers to the "mercy seat" in the temple on which blood was sprinkled through an incense haze, and at which place God's merciful forgiveness was granted on the Day of Atonement. Now the connotations of "mercy seat" can work in the direction of appeasing wrath, should one correlate the mercy seat with the theme of wrath in 1:18–3:20 (see more below) and with the theodicy concerns of 3:25-26, or it can work in the direction of expiating sin, should one focus on 3:23. I see no reason to deny either element from the evocation of "mercy seat." However one construes this phrase, God's right-making occurs by humans being in union with Christ through faith.

Seventh, central to this gracious work of God is that it is accomplished through the life-giving death of Jesus Christ ("blood"), whose incarnation creates identification with humans in their cracked condition. And, as if to anticipate Anselm himself (and often neglected by many atonement theorists), *eighth*, God's right-making is done in such a way that preserves two things: God's own attribute of being faithful to his own justice and God's own intent of "right-making." That is, the atoning work of God is done in such a way that God neither broaches his own justice nor fails to show mercy. On the "mercy seat" known as Jesus Christ's death on the cross, Paul is saying, love and justice lock themselves in gracious embrace and God rids his people of the sin problem.

Impossible as it is to summarize Paul, even Paul in a few verses of soteriological flurry such as we find in Romans 3:21-26, what we have is this: cracked Eikons—Jew or Gentile, male or female, slave or free—are declared and made right with God, are forgiven of their sins and sinfulness, and the wrath of God from 1:18–3:20 is diverted by being absorbed in Christ's death. Because God is gracious and merciful in sending his Son, Jesus Christ, to the world to identify with us so that he can die (give his life) with us and for us, those who are "in Christ" can be ushered into a community where things are put to rights. "Being made right," "being redeemed," and "finding mercy" are accomplished not by observing Torah but by orienting one's trust in Jesus Christ, the one who died for others and who incarnates God's faithfulness to his covenant promises.

Two questions beg for further answers in this context and from what Paul implies in his theology of the death of Christ—the questions of justification (or "right-making") and wrath.

Justification and Wrath

What does "justification" mean? That is the ten-million-dollar question today, and there is insufficient space here to explore the discussion.[8] Before we say anything else, "right-making" or "justification" is only one metaphor (and it is at least a metaphor) among three in this text, the others being "redemption" and "mercy seat." Nor is it the central metaphor in Pauline theology. Nor can it be dismissed as "just" a metaphor.

"Justification" is God's merciful act of declaring, in the imagery of a judge in a courtroom, people right. This defines who the people of God are. Justification involves wiping sins away and creating a new people in Christ. But, to back up to one of our earlier concerns, this act of God's forensic judgment is the mercy of God in action, not the twisting and fighting of one of God's attributes against another—nor is it the Father's judgment because his Son has somehow stepped in and changed the mind of the Father. Justification, God's declaring and making things right, emerges always and forever from the mercy of God and God's intention to redeem his people from their cracked Eikonic condition. And this all happens because Jesus Christ is the second Adam/Israel who lives obediently before God and absorbs the curse of death by plunging into its central forces and coming out the other side (resurrection) victoriously, creating a stream of grace for all who will put their eyes of faith on him.

Which means that we also have to ask this set of questions: From what are we "justified"? From what are we "redeemed"? With what does the "mercy seat" act deal? There is a short answer and a long answer. The short answer is "sin"—as is seen in 3:23 and 3:25. The long answer, if one takes into consideration the context from 1:18–3:20, is "wrath" and "death." Within God's own creational intent is human freedom; within that freedom is the human choice to go against God and to sin; within that choice in freedom is death as the inevitable consequence of sin; within the freedom of God is wrath, or God's jealous displeasure, with Eikons going their own way into diminishment as Eikons. God's wrath appears no fewer than thirty times in the New Testament, two-thirds of which are found in Romans and Revelation.

In nearly a decade of serious thinking, exploring, and reading about atonement, I have encountered many who are repulsed by the concept of wrath, and I am persuaded that the reason most are repulsed has to do not with the way the Bible deals with the divine response to the sacred violation of God's gracious love (wrath) in historical judgment, but with the way wrath is spoken of by Christians—mostly preachers, evangelists, and parents. If wrath, according to the Bible, is God's jealous[9] response to the violation of his love that manifests itself in (mostly historical) judgment, and if wrath is what humans do to themselves as they diminish their Eikonic glory, and if in so using such a term we can keep from bipolarizing God's nature and the persons of the Trinity, perhaps we will find yet another way to bring wrath back into the discussion.

Ever since C. H. Dodd, "wrath" has found many who argue that it means the impersonal, inevitable consequences of sin.[10] That is, it is not the momentary, personal reaction of a holy God to specific sins, but instead a system God has established: an impersonal cause and effect, an impersonal establishment of the laws of consequences. Dig a hole, and you'll fall into it. There remains one fundamental problem for this so-called impersonal view of wrath: *Who* established the impersonal, inevitable consequence factor? If God is the one who established this so-called impersonal system of consequences, then one cannot either make it *im*personal (for God is personal in all that God does) or somehow separate it from God (for it is, after all, *God* who made the system of consequences). In my judgment, the path of impersonal wrath is a blind alley. The wrath of God is God's jealousy when Eikons walk away from God.

I find that most will embrace wrath as Tom Wright puts it:

> Paul's whole theology, not least the expression of it in Romans, is grounded in the robust and scripturally rooted view that the creator is neither a tyrannical despot nor an indulgent, *laissez-faire* absentee landlord, nor yet, for that matter, the mere inner or spiritual dimension of all that is. God is the creator and lover of the world. This God has a passionate concern for creation, and humans in particular, that will tolerate nothing less than the best for them.
>
> The result is "wrath"—not just a settled attitude of hostility toward idolatry and immorality, but actions that follow from such an attitude when the one to whom it belongs is the sovereign creator.[11]

If they will not agree with Wright, perhaps they will with Paul Fiddes, the Oxford theologian:

> If God is passionately involved in the life of his creation...then he is involved in the process of natural justice. He consents in an *active* and personal way to the structure of justice in the world, and so this consent can truly be called the 'wrath' of God against sin which spoils his work.
>
> There is no conflict in God. In his love God passionately desires to bring all humankind into fellowship with himself. In his justice God underwrites the consequences of sin, though (as the Old Testament prophets make clear) he does so with an agony in his heart.[12]

God's wrath is God's jealousy at work to woo back cracked Eikons to God's love. Exodus 34:14: "for you shall worship no other god, because the LORD, whose name is Jealous, is a jealous God." Even more completely: "Now I will restore the fortunes of Jacob, and have mercy on the whole house of Israel; and I will be jealous for my holy name" (Ezek. 39:25). The theme of God as a jealous God occurs often in the Old Testament: Exodus 20:5; Deuteronomy 4:24; 5:9; 6:15; 32:16, 19, 21; Joshua 24:19; Psalm 79:5; Ezekiel 36:6; Zechariah 8:2.

What needs to be observed in Romans 3:21-26 is that God's act of grace, the death of Christ as the mercy seat, is directed toward humans who have walked away from God. God, in his jealousy, warns them of the danger as God seeks them out: "While we still were sinners Christ died for us" (Rom. 5:8). (By the way, this means that atonement is at some level the act of God, not of changing his mind but of changing the "status" or "relationship" of Eikons to God by carving a path through sin and death into the glorious light of God's eternal life and presence.)

Wrath, however, is not the only point of the cross, and any dwelling on this fails to deliver the goods of atonement. Wrath is the other side of God's love, God's jealousy, and it is God's love that prompts God to send his Son to restore creation.

Conclusion

I suggest that we see the achievement of the cross in three expressions: Jesus dies "with us"—entering into our evil and our sin and our suffering to subvert it and create a new way; Jesus dies "instead of us"—he enters into *our* sin, *our* wrath, and *our* death; and Jesus dies "for us"—his death forgives our sin, "declares us right," absorbs the wrath of God against us, and creates new life where there was once only death.

Not only is this death saving, this same death becomes the paradigm for an entirely new existence that is shaped, as Luther said of theology and life, by the cross. A life shaped by the cross is a life bent on dying daily to self in order to love God, self, others, and the world. And a life shaped by the cross sees in the cross God becoming the victim, identifying with the victim, suffering injustice, and shaping a cruciform pattern of life for all who would follow Jesus. The cross reshapes all of life.

CHAPTER
TEN

ATONING MOMENTS: EASTER AND PENTECOST

While the outpouring of the Holy Spirit on the day of Pentecost is pictured as the event that gave birth to the church as a self-conscious fellowship, the transformation of Jesus' disciples from a terrified, hopeless, disappointed band to the bold preachers of Jesus as Messiah and the agent of salvation was caused by his resurrection from the dead.

—G. E. Ladd[1]

A biblical theory of atonement does not stop at the cross, even if it views the incarnate life of Jesus and everything else through the piercing image of the cross. Several texts bring home the fundamental reality that, without the resurrection, atonement is incomplete. We need to begin with this: the point of the resurrection is more than hope for those who fear death, for those who are on the verge of death, or even for those who long to be reunited with loved ones. Resurrection, leading as it does to eternal life, is more than the hope for what Tom Wright in numerous settings calls "life after life after death."

What, then, is the resurrection all about? If the death of Christ wipes away sin, the resurrection of Christ *makes all things new*. Resurrection is about new creation. A theory of atonement that does not flow into the resurrection is an atonement that rids one of the sin problem but does not transform life and this world. Stopping that flow of life from God into God's people is the abortion of full atonement. To extend my earlier image, many choose to leave the resurrection and Pentecost clubs at home when playing the atonement game. The bag is incomplete until both are carried.

Romans 4:25: Eikons Recreated

Perhaps it needs to be restated that the resurrection of Jesus is central to the gospel. Resurrection, to be sure, is the actual enlivening of Jesus' body, as Paul goes to great pains to show (1 Cor. 15:35-49), and without that resurrection, there is no hope before God, before self, before others, and before the world. As Paul states it: "If Christ has not been raised, your faith is futile and you are still in your sins" (15:17). A real resurrection, then, is at the foundation of the gospel, at the foundation of the atonement, and without resurrection—Jesus' real, physical body coming back to life as a new glorious body, Jesus' "life after life after death"—there is no forgiveness of sins. Jesus' resurrection severs the chains to death, gives a person new life, and sets that person free.

A complete theory of atonement will press beyond the cross to discover that the resurrection creates new life beyond death. Why? Because it is in the resurrection that atonement accomplishes its final designs. The resurrection creates new life in the here and now for the community of faith as well as in the there and then for that same community. As Jonathan Wilson sums it up, "In Christ as victor, we see God as our warrior, our conqueror, our liberator, who reveals our victimization and captivity, defeats our enemy, destroys our prison, and shatters our chains to free us and bring us home to live for eternity."[2]

Here is another club that must be used in the game called atonement: atonement is not only about removing sin but also about setting those chained to sin free, about *Christus Victor*, Christ the victor who liberates his people to be God's people on earth.

Resurrection and Justification

Most of the time we connect justification to the cross, and at the end of chapter 7 I made that point clear. The victory of justification, though, requires the resurrection. Abraham, Paul says, believed in God and it was "reckoned to him as righteousness," and in so trusting Abraham becomes the prototypical believer. But notice these words: "It will be reckoned to us who believe in him who raised Jesus our Lord from the dead, who was handed over to death for our trespasses and *was raised for our justification*" (Rom. 4:24b-25, emphasis added).[3] Forgiveness and justification, Paul says, maybe are prepared for in the cross but neither is fully effective until the resurrection. Why? Because for Paul the atonement is a comprehensive work of not only wiping the slate clean of sins but also of restoring cracked Eikons by gifting them with the life of God so they can participate in God's life. Atonement is both elimination of the problem and the enablement of a new life. And the direction of that new life is ecclesial: resurrection creates a new community for all.

Resurrection and the Gentiles

In Romans 3:21-26, where Paul puts on the table the resolution of the conflict expressed in 1:18–3:20, an overlooked but important element of the resolution is that the "work of Christ" is for "*all* who believe" (3:22). The sweep of history that occupies Paul's attention in 3:25 speaks to the same theme: God will be faithful to his covenant, God will bring about what he promised, and *God will bring together Jews and Gentiles.* How? Through a death-and-resurrection event. Notice these words from Romans 10:9-10: "because if you confess with your lips that Jesus is Lord and believe in your heart that *God raised him from the dead*, you will be *saved.* For one believes with the heart and so is *justified*, and one confesses with the mouth and so is *saved*" (emphasis added). And a few lines later Paul makes it clear that he has in mind the inclusion of Gentiles and Jews in this resurrection work of God: "for there is no distinction between Jew and Greek" (10:12). Resurrection, justification, and the inclusion of Gentiles are connected points on Paul's map.

Without the resurrection, the boundary line between Jews and Gentiles remains standing; with the resurrection, a transnational community is formed. When resurrection is integrated into how we understand the atonement, we quickly find ourselves discussing the inclusive community of faith.

New Creation

Resurrection for Paul *will* take place as a "transformation" (cf. Phil. 3:10-11, 21), but that transformation *is already taking place* as transform*ing.* Again, we observe the *ongoing* glorifying of believers indwelled by the Spirit in 2 Corinthians 3:18: "And all of us, with unveiled faces, seeing the glory of the Lord as though reflected in a mirror, are being transformed into the same image from one degree of glory to another; for this comes from the Lord, the Spirit."

Resurrection power is at work, already, in the believers in Jesus because they have the Spirit. The threat of daily external decay and death is met by daily inner renewal through the Spirit. Herein lies the power of the resurrection at work in the ecclesial community of faith. Romans 6:1-11 follows the same line: co-crucifixion leads to co-resurrection, and co-resurrection leads to moral transformation in the present age. One more passage that puts this together is 2 Corinthians 5:15, which tells us that we are to live "for him who died and was raised" for us, and such a living is possible because for everyone who is "in Christ, there is a new creation" (5:17). That is, those who are "in Christ" find themselves in a new order of the new day when Christ makes all things new *by virtue of his resurrection*. Once again we see that all this occurs in our union with Christ.

We could develop such a theme at length. Enough has been presented to draw the important conclusion that atonement is effected through the death and resurrection of Christ because the design of atonement concerns the restoration of cracked Eikons in the context of a community of faith wherein God "makes things new" as continually renewed Eikons live out the will of God in the here and now. The resurrection gives a person hope and a new life.

Three moments of atonement so far have been incarnation, death, and resurrection. The final "moment" concerns Pentecost, an event that is often overlooked in theories of atonement.

Pentecost: Acts 2 and Eikons Empowered

The story the early Christians told is that Jesus lived, Jesus died, Jesus was raised, and Jesus was exalted into the heavens, from which place he sent the Holy Spirit on the day of Pentecost. Jesus' life, death, resurrection, and Pentecost are integrally related. Together they accomplish forgiveness, new creation, and empowerment. Before we get to Acts 2, let us observe the magnificent creed-like statement tucked into Peter's first letter (3:18-22), and observe that Peter sees God's atoning work in each of these moments. The comprehensive theme:

> For Christ also suffered for sins once for all, the righteous for the unrighteous, in order to bring you to God.

The moments:

> He was put to death in the flesh, but made alive in the spirit ... through the resurrection of Jesus Christ, who has gone into heaven and is at the right hand of God, with angels, authorities, and powers made subject to him.

Here Peter sees God leading humans into the very presence of God through the incarnate life, the suffering death and the resurrection of

Jesus, and the empowerment of the Spirit and Jesus' ascension.[4] Several themes capture the impact of Pentecost for atonement.

New Covenant

The first theme is *new covenant*. "Covenant" is not a common category through which the NT writers, apart from the writer of Hebrews, processed their thinking. Its rarity in the NT (33 times, with about half in Hebrews) surprises many of us since we have been taught to read the Bible in "covenant" terms, and it appears in gold letters on many of our Bibles: the Old and New "Testaments" or "Covenants."

Still, the experience of the Spirit at Pentecost (Acts 2) opens up Christian covenant thinking: the gift of the Spirit triggered the memory of Jeremiah 31:31-33, in which Jeremiah's predictions of the new covenant are recorded.

> The days are surely coming, says the LORD, when I will make a new covenant with the house of Israel and the house of Judah. It will not be like the covenant that I made with their ancestors when I took them by the hand to bring them out of the land of Egypt—a covenant that they broke, though I was their husband, says the LORD. But this is the covenant that I will make with the house of Israel after those days, says the LORD: I will put my law within them, and I will write it on their hearts; and I will be their God, and they shall be my people.

At Pentecost, the Christians who had seen what happened suddenly knew that they were a part of the restoration of Israel and the recreation of a new people of God. The covenant Israel had broken was being renewed by the gift of the Spirit, who was written into the very heart of the believer. This time, unlike the experience of the older covenant, the covenant would be unbreakable, internal, and democratic. This new covenant issues in the forgiveness of sins and peace for all people.[5]

The essence of new covenant thinking is the conviction that the Spirit of God was at work in a new and powerful way—restoring the covenant, renewing people, and recreating the community of faith.

Ecclesial Formation

Second, and by far the most noteworthy feature of Pentecost, is the *ecclesial* shape of the work of God: at Pentecost the Holy Spirit is poured out in order *to create a universal community of faith that worships, fellowships, and missionally expands.*[6] Before another word be said, notice the essence of this act of God: Pentecost comes not simply to regenerate individual Eikons but to recreate *an ecclesial community* of faith in which the will of God manifests itself in worship, fellowship, and the *missio Dei.* We find at Pentecost the divine intention of God's atoning work: the creation of a community of faith in which and through which cracked Eikons will be restored to union with God and communion with others for the good of the world.

Once again we face a central feature of this book's thesis about the atonement: atonement cannot be restricted to saving individuals. When it is, it destroys the fabric of the biblical story. That fabric is the community of faith, and atonement is designed to create that community. Nothing makes that more obvious than the gift of the Spirit in Acts 2.

The missional work of the Pentecostal community emerged from its capacity to speak in other tongues so that all might be included (Acts 2:4). Notice how Peter understood Pentecost: he claimed that this act of God fulfilled Joel 2:28-32. What did that text speak of? Clearly, it spoke of God's sending of the Spirit *to democratize the people of God as an act of apocalyptic judgment on unjust rulers.*[7] Notice how this quotation by Peter puts together two central themes: the Spirit for *all* and judgment on *injustice.* We need to think about this more than we do, for once again our tendency is to see Pentecost as an act for individuals. But for Peter the gift of the Spirit is *cosmic.*

The text from Joel begins with the Spirit coming upon *all*: "Even upon my slaves, both men and women, in those days I will pour out my Spirit; and they shall prophesy." And then it continues with apocalyptic language that is code language for *political disaster,* the kind of disaster that brings to expression God's wrath against injustices and unjust rulers. This language, contrary to a well-known set of novels dealing with eschatology, is not about astral portents that happen in the sky and affect planet earth, but is instead metaphorical, apocalyptic language that images political disaster. Here is Acts 2:19-21:

> And I will show portents in the heaven above
>> and signs on the earth below,
>>> blood, and fire, and smoky mist.
> The sun shall be turned to darkness
>> and the moon to blood,
>>> before the coming of the Lord's great and glorious day.
> Then everyone who calls on the name of the Lord shall be saved.

These signs are not cosmic disturbances that will upset photosynthesis and water flow; instead, these images stand for God's act of judgment on the wicked rulers who sent Jesus to a cruel death.

I do not know that anyone has said this, so let me offer a suggestion: Pentecost is both justification and judgment. In this one act at Pentecost (1) the people of God, in God's act of justifying and making his judgment clear, receive the power of the Holy Spirit to create a community wherein the will of God can be done, and (2) that new community creation is *at the same time* a judgment on the unjust rulers of this world.

If we have a broad enough canvass for atonement, we can see the themes of atonement everywhere: Jesus as God's agent of redemption, as well as Jesus' death, resurrection, and vindication, and Pentecost—and along with those themes the universalizing and democratizing promises that are embodied in a new community of faith—and along with these the establishment of justice in this world.

Power to Transcend

Third, a significant feature of the Pentecostal Spirit is the *power to transcend, to break down boundaries, and to expand the people of God*. Acts 1–15 records the history of a Jewish-Christian community of faith knocking down boundaries to expand into a more inclusive community of faith, working out the practice of Jesus at the table and learning how the covenant faithfulness of God would work out the universal redemptive designs—first to the Samaritans, then to the Ethiopian eunuch, then through Peter into the Gentile world, and finally with Paul into a full-scale missional focus on Gentiles. If anything is certain, the earliest Jewish-Christian community did not know what to make of this expansiveness of the community of faith, but they knew the Spirit was giving it power to overcome their own hesitations. "God doesn't give people the Holy Spirit," Tom Wright says, "in order to let them enjoy the spiritual equivalent of a day at Disneyland." No, he says,

> the point of the Spirit is to enable those who follow Jesus to take into all the world the news that he is Lord, that he has won the victory over the forces of evil, that a new world has opened up, and that we are to help make it happen.[8]

Fellowshipping Body

Fourth, the Spirit who empowers the saints is the Spirit that makes them a *fellowshipping* body—and here we think of 1 Corinthians 12–14 with Paul's potent image of Christians being body parts who are in need of one another so that the redemptive work of God can be accomplished. The singular power for such redemptive work through *a unified and complementary body* is the Spirit:

> Now there are varieties of gifts, but the same **Spirit**; and there are varieties of services, but the same Lord; and there are varieties of activities, but it is the same God who activates all of them in everyone. To each is given the manifestation of the **Spirit** for the common good. To one is given through the **Spirit** the utterance of wisdom, and to another the utterance of knowledge according to the same **Spirit**, to another faith by the same **Spirit**, to another gifts of healing by the one **Spirit**, to another the working of miracles, to another prophecy, to another the discernment of spirits, to another various kinds of tongues, to another the interpretation of tongues. All these are activated by one and the same **Spirit**, who allots to each one individually just as the **Spirit** chooses.
>
> For just as the body is one and has many members, and all the members of the body, though many, are one body, so it is with Christ. For in the one **Spirit** we were all baptized into one body—Jews or Greeks, slaves or free— and we were all made to drink of one **Spirit**. (1 Cor. 12:4-13)

For Paul, the unity of the body of Christ is a recreation of the Spirit of God, the new creation itself, and through that Spirit the community is empowered to praise God, fellowship with one another, and carry on missional work.

We dare not forget Pentecost when we speak of atonement. Pentecost makes things right by creating the new covenant, filling all with the Spirit, and creating the ecclesial community and enabling it to live in love with one another. Put differently, Pentecost empowers all to be restored in all four directions: with God, with self, with others, and with the world. Pentecost crystallizes the intent of God's atoning work.

Conclusion

We need now to sum up what we have claimed in Part 2 of this book as we seek, by canvassing all that is involved in atonement, an image or a comprehensive category that does justice to the biblical concept of atonement.

God designed the moments of atonement to deal a deathblow to evil and therefore to restore cracked Eikons to be Christ-like Eikons by drawing them into union with God and communion with others. Atonement, then, includes the incarnation, death, and resurrection of Jesus, and the gift of the Spirit at Pentecost. And what we see in each of these is that the atonement intends principally to create an ecclesial community of faith wherein the will of God is actualized—that is, where evil comes and finds no open door and where justice swamps the place. I quote Jürgen Moltmann:

> Through *the forgiveness of sins* the gospel breaks through the compulsive acts of sinners which are the enemies of life, cutting sinners loose from sin, and creating the possibility of "conversion," a turn to life. Through *the justification of sinners*, the gospel brings men and women who are closed in upon themselves into the open love of God. Through *rebirth from the Spirit*, it brings people who have been subject to death into touch with the eternal source of life, setting them in the closer framework of the rebirth of human community and against the wider horizon of the rebirth of the cosmos.[9]

We began this section of *A Community Called Atonement* by inquiring into which metaphor is best. We have now sorted out those individual metaphors and we have looked at the major moments of atonement. But we are now facing a major issue: the images of atonement in the New Testament are not systematic theologies but stories. And not only are they stories, they are particular stories that dip into the great story of Israel and bring that story into new shape with a new form and with new content. So, before we give ourselves permission to synthesize these metaphors into a comprehensive category, we need to look at three of these stories. We will look at the story of Jesus, of Paul, and of some early theologians. With metaphors, moments, and story on the table, we will finally be able to offer a comprehensive category—one that both transcends the individual metaphors and that respects the contours of each metaphor as shaped by the various stories in which they find themselves.

PART THREE

Atonement as Story: Whose Story?

C H A P T E R
E L E V E N

THE STORY OF JESUS: PASSOVER

We must, therefore, look considerably deeper for the reasons for the "odd circumstance" before us, namely, the absence of a developed theory of the death of Christ, in any way comparable to the Christological theories of the first five or six centuries.

—John McIntyre[1]

Most people don't ask the question that we will discuss in this chapter: What did *Jesus* think of his death? Most simply assume—and I hear it all the time—that Jesus thought what *they themselves* believe about the death of Christ. In other words, some historians and theologians think Jesus' death had nothing to do with the plan of God but that Jesus died a tragic death because he had the courage to preach the kingdom of God. Some thinkers, at the very opposite end of the issue, assume that Jesus knew from the very beginning that he was appointed to die and that his death was the whole purpose of his mission. There are lots of scholars who fit somewhere between these two approaches.

Jesus and His Death

This section reflects more than six years of reflection on my part about what Jesus thought of his death. My book *Jesus and His Death*[2] explores the issues involved in more detail and with a greater emphasis. Here are a few preliminary observations. The *first* thing we need to admit is that what Jesus thought and what Paul or the writer to the Hebrews or Peter thought are not always identical. When we begin to make Jesus think like the later New Testament writers we fail to see the importance of how New Testament thinking about Jesus' death developed. The *second* thing we need to admit is that the bulk of critical scholars today believe that Jesus *never* interpreted his death as atoning because the evidence that suggests such is judged not to have been said by Jesus. Many think that Jesus probably saw his death coming down the road. "How could he not have?" they ask. But to think that Jesus thought his death was atoning or that he actually believed that his death would save is simply off the map for many critical scholars. *Jesus and His Death* was an attempt to get that discussion back on the table for historical Jesus experts.

A *third* observation: the earliest theologians did believe Jesus' death was atoning. It is OK, so it is sometimes argued, for them to think this way even if Jesus didn't think that way. Why? Because Christian theology is an ongoing, reflective activity led by the Spirit in the church. Any person who reads the New Testament fairly knows that Paul makes more of the atoning death of Jesus than anyone else, excluding perhaps the writer to the Hebrews. There is nothing but virtue in admitting that the New Testament really does show this kind of development. But, still, many of us are more than a little bothered to think that a central, if not *the* central, belief of Christians—that Jesus' death was atoning—was not something Jesus himself believed.

I wish to make this *fourth* point: as often as not, it is more than difficult to prove what Jesus did or didn't say *if* we limit ourselves to historical methods.[3] Regardless of how difficult it might be to prove such things, there are two observations that lead me to think that Jesus did interpret his death as atoning. I begin with this observation: from the moment John the Baptist's head was decapitated, Jesus must have thought about the likelihood of his own death. I consider it impossible for Jesus not to have wondered if he might not also die prematurely. There are numerous sayings of Jesus that show that he expected to die prematurely. Thus, "the Son of Man is to be betrayed into human hands, and they will kill him, and three days after being killed, he will rise again" (Mark 9:31). Another saying that reflects the sort of thing Jesus said often enough to make an impression can be found in Luke 13:31-33:

> At that very hour some Pharisees came and said to him, "Get away from here, for Herod wants to kill you." He said to them, "Go and tell that fox for me, 'Listen, I am casting out demons and performing cures today and tomorrow, and on the third day I finish my work. Yet today, tomorrow, and the next day I must be on my way, because it is impossible for a prophet to be killed outside of Jerusalem.'"

A second observation is that it is impossible for someone like Jesus to have known he was going to die prematurely and not to have thought about it and made sense of that death in light of Scripture. There is evidence that Jesus did exactly that—twice. In both Mark 10:45 and 14:24 Jesus clarified the meaning of his death as atoning, which leads to the necessary admission that the nature and centrality of the Christian belief in Jesus' atoning death is at least partly wrapped in a conviction that God's Spirit directed the leaders of the church to develop what Jesus said—and I think it can be shown that those developments are organic developments of what Jesus himself did say.

In what follows I ask two simple questions: How did Jesus interpret his own death? Which of Israel's scriptural stories did his interpretation reflect?

Jesus and Passover

Jesus found the story of his own death in Passover and the exodus. It is not possible here to examine each and every issue, but there are two texts in the Gospels in which Jesus actually "interprets" his death—or, better yet, places his impending death into the story of God's kingdom work with Israel. They are Mark 14:24 and Mark 10:45.

The Last Supper

Of the two texts that deal specifically with how Jesus understood his own death, I will begin with Mark 14:24 because it is the clearest: "He said to them, 'This is my blood of the covenant, which is poured out for many.'" It was at a Passover week meal, what Christians now celebrate as a memorial meal in the Last Supper or the Lord's Supper (Mark 14:17-25), that Jesus offered a definitive interpretation of his death. His words over the bread and wine set the stage for a variety of explorations by later New Testament authors. Once again, Jesus "storifies" his own death by setting that death in the context of *Passover and exodus.* There are many debatable issues, and I wish merely to state where I am standing.

One issue is whether or not the Last Supper is the Passover meal proper. In spite of the rather casual assumption many make that the Last Supper was the Passover meal itself, the Gospels seem to differ here. I think it is more probable that the Last Supper is not the Passover meal proper, but instead a Passover-like meal the night before the Passover meal. The reason I think this is that John explicitly claims that Jesus died when the Passover lambs were being slain. John 19:14 says, just before they led Jesus out to be crucified, "Now it was the day of Preparation for the Passover." And, after his crucifixion, John 19:31 says this: "Since it was the day of Preparation, the Jews did not want the bodies left on the cross during the sabbath." Some disagree with me on this and think John is speaking of a Sabbath preparation only. There is enough debate here to keep us from getting too dogmatic about our conclusions. It does not make that much difference, for however we take it, Passover was an eight-day event and not simply a one-night meal. Every meal during Passover would be Passover-like. It might be worth observing here that there is no mention of eating the lamb in the Last Supper. I find that absence telling. Why would Jesus not have connected the Last Supper with eating the lamb that was slain instead of the bread? Probably, I think, because there was no lamb at the meal.

During the meal, Jesus interprets the bread (not lamb) and wine as his body and his blood. No one can dispute that Jesus anticipates his own death in such language. What amazes is that he gives the symbols of his death to his followers and asks them to eat and drink them—both body and blood. No one should accuse either Jesus or his followers of some crude cannibalism. Instead, Jesus is asking his followers to participate in his death. But rather than dying with him on the cross, he asks that they merely ingest bread and wine to identify themselves in the story of Jesus and so learn to participate in his death by faith. Jesus *identifies with* them in his death and *incorporates them into his death*. In fact, he dies *instead of them* as a substitutionary act. He exhorts them to participate in the *benefits* of his death by eating and drinking.

Benefits

What do Jesus' followers get by ingesting Jesus' body and blood? The narratives differ in words and details, but the Gospels agree that Jesus is somehow dying *for them* (Mark 14:24).

Each of the traditions says that such an act establishes a *covenant* (Mark 14:24; Matt. 26:28; Luke 22:20; 1 Cor. 11:25). This meal becomes for the Christians what the covenant ceremony was for Israel (Exod. 19–24). In this meal Jesus establishes a new ecclesial community by his death and the disciples become part of that ecclesial body by ingesting his body and blood.

And Matthew—but only Matthew—adds in 26:28 "for the *forgiveness* of sins," which indicates both a personal resolution of one's relationship with God through the Torah (guilt) and the restoration of Israel (the corporate sense of forgiveness).

Liberation

Now we must back up to see the Last Supper in its historical context and in light of the problem (sin, the cracked Eikon) that it resolves, and this step is necessary because of the tendency to impose later understandings of Jesus' death onto Jesus himself. We are asking how he understood his death as presented in the Gospels. Passover and the exodus are front, back, left, right, and center events to commemorate one thing: *liberation* from Egypt. As such, Passover became the event of the year for Israel to remember God's faithful ransoming, rescuing, saving work. And Passover was a reminder of God's faithful promise to be King and Savior of Israel. This can only mean that the event was fraught with political implications for Roman rulers as Israel thought of what God might again do for Israel. Of all the high holidays in Israel, Passover threatened the *pax Romana* and the stability of the land of Israel.

And now we get to what I think is the most important question that, when answered, unlocks the door to how Jesus understood his own death.

Why This Night? Or, Why Not Yom Kippur?

We need to reconsider why it was that Jesus chose *Passover* (a night of celebrating and remembering liberation) rather than *Yom Kippur*, the Day of Atonement (a day of affliction and a day when sins were atoned for). Why does he choose this night to take his stand for what his death meant? Why die on Passover instead of Yom Kippur? Details about these feasts can be found by reading Leviticus 16 and 23. It could be that Passover was a pilgrim festival, and hence attended by more, and Yom Kippur was not; Jesus could have been thinking of the larger crowd. From the "triumphal entry" forward, Jesus was aware of mounting opposition to what he was doing. That he stayed the course is significant. He could have escaped from Jerusalem and returned to Galilee in the quiet of the night. Aware of the opening chasm of death before him, Jesus chose to stay and he chose to die.

Again, we ask: Why choose Passover for his death?

We answer that by answering this question: What did *death at Passover* do? Passover involved the death of a lamb and the smearing of a lamb's blood with the hyssop branch on the door; the blood protected from God's wrath and liberated Israel. If this is what Passover was about, then this is what Jesus was doing: "storifying" his own death at Passover, claiming that his followers, by ingesting his body and blood, were "smearing" blood on themselves to protect themselves from the judgment of God against the oppressive, violent, and power-mongering leaders of Israel and Rome who were oppressing God's good people. We need to recall that Jesus had just announced (read Mark 13) that judgment would shortly come to Jerusalem. God's wrath is here understood in concrete, historical terms: judgment against sin and systemic violence in the historical order.

If we think about what this might have meant to the first followers of Jesus, we could conclude this: the Last Supper was an act of liberation from Rome and Israel's unjust leaders and the claim that those who "ingest" Jesus will be protected from them and liberated to live in the kingdom of God. By choosing Passover instead of Yom Kippur to explain his death, Jesus chooses the images of divine protection and liberation. He offers himself—in death—to absorb the judgment of God on behalf of his followers so he can save his people from their sins. His is the blood of the lamb that will secure his followers for the kingdom of God.

No one would argue that this is all there is to the death of Jesus, but one must begin right here: Jesus' act at the Last Supper declares that his death is atoning, that his blood is like the Passover blood, that his blood absorbs the judgment of God against sin and systemic violence, that his death will save and liberate his followers from their own sins, and that his death will create the new covenant community around him.

Mark 10:45

We turn now back to Mark 10:45: "For the Son of Man came not to be served but to serve, and to give his life a ransom for many." Everything here hinges on the last three words: "ransom for many." With Mark 10:45, once again, we are dealing with a set of words best understood by beginning with the Passover sacrifice, in which Israelite fathers sacrificed a lamb and then smeared its blood on the lintels of the door. These slain lambs, in effect, became a "ransom" price for Israel to escape both the avenging angel and the clutches of Pharaoh and the Egyptians. I'm not sure that the words of Mark

10:45 can be limited to Passover, but they are surely connected to Passover. We can also connect this term "ransom" to Isaiah 43:3-7:

> For I am the LORD your God,
>   the Holy One of Israel, your Savior.
> I give Egypt *as your ransom,*
>   Ethiopia and Seba *in exchange for you.*
> Because you are precious in my sight,
>   and honored, and I love you,
> *I give people in return for you,*
>   *nations in exchange for your life.*
> Do not fear, for I am with you;
>   I will bring your offspring from the east,
>   and from the west I will gather you;
> I will say to the north, "Give them up,"
>   and to the south, "Do not withhold;
> bring my sons from far away
>   and my daughters from the end of the earth—
> everyone who is called by my name,
>   whom I created for my glory,
>   whom I formed and made." (emphasis added)

Here the image of "ransom" is explained: Egypt's and Ethiopia's and Seba's subjugation pays the price for Israel to be released from captivity in Babylon. If this is in the background of Mark 10:45, then Jesus sees his death as the "ransom price" to release his followers from their own captivity.

We can also connect "ransom" to lines in Isaiah 52:13–53:12, where we find a similar meaning: as Israel was in captivity in Babylon, so the servant's "ransom price," his suffering and death, will be the ransom price for the release and liberation of Israel so they can return to the land. Notice these lines from Isaiah's famous Servant Song:

> He was despised and rejected by others;
>   a man of suffering and acquainted with infirmity;
> and as one from whom others hide their faces
>   he was despised, and we held him of no account.

> But he was wounded for our transgressions,
>   crushed for our iniquities;
> upon him was the punishment that made us whole,
>   and by his bruises we are healed.

The righteous one, my servant, *shall make many righteous,*
and he shall bear their iniquities.
Therefore I will allot him a portion with the great,
and he shall divide the spoil with the strong;
because *he poured out himself to death,*
and was numbered with the transgressors;
yet he bore the sin of many,
and made intercession for the transgressors. (emphasis added)

The singular theme of these verses in Isaiah is simple: *a death, understood as a ransom price, leads to the liberation of others.* This is what Jesus is saying in Mark 10:45. We are dealing here, then, with a metaphor of *liberation*—as Israel was set free, so the "many" will be set free. But from what? The contexts in Exodus and Isaiah provide the answer: captivity and oppression.

We should observe, then, the context for Mark's saying in Mark 10:35-45: Jesus is criticizing both the Roman practice of power and the disciples' yearnings for power and control. Jesus says he has died to liberate them from that kind of sinful, systemic, unjust empire. Their desires to rule merely parrot the Roman Empire's ideology. They are called to something different. In fact, they are "ransomed" from that. They will be set free, as the Israelites were, from oppression and oppressing so they can live, as the *Benedictus* anticipated, in the land and worship God as Israel ought.

The first understanding of Jesus is a complex story of both personal redemption and ecclesial recreation: it is the story of liberation from sin and oppression so God's people can live in the new community just as they were designed by God to live. Atonement and kingdom emerge into a coherent whole: Jesus' mission to establish the kingdom, a society in which God's will would be done, is why he dies. He understands his death as the atoning work of God to create a society, an ecclesial community, in which God's will could be done. He came to liberate his people from their sins and the world's unjust systems. He accomplishes that liberation by entering into enemy territory (sin and enslavement), by being captured to the point of death *instead of* and *for the benefit of* others, and by escaping from that captivity through the resurrection. This is what the "ransom price" was all about. By ingesting that bread and wine, the disciples confess their complicity in sin and find that Jesus' own death is offered instead of theirs. The logic of Passover is the logic, in historical terms, of a substitutionary death that absorbs the judgment of God, protects those who ingest the bread and wine, and sets them free.

From Jesus to Paul

Jesus' own story, the story of Passover and exodus, was not the only one the early Christians were to tell about Jesus' death. What needs to be observed here is absolutely critical for the direction emerging theology wants us to walk: *the language even of Jesus was not privileged.* First let me elaborate and then offer an explanation. Paul evidently was under no compulsion to use Jesus' "kingdom" language. The apostle John wasn't either; he turned the rhetoric of Jesus about "kingdom" into the rhetoric of "eternal life." The writer of Hebrews explored Jesus' redemptive work through the imagery of the temple and the priesthood, and he felt no compulsion to use Jesus' or Paul's language for the work of God. No one seemed tied to the language of Jesus.

We can now connect what we have said about Jesus' own Passover/exodus story to Romans 3:21-26. In essence, the scope of "wrath" in Romans 1:18–3:20 is an organic development of what Jesus means by eating and drinking to be protected from (by absorption of) God's judgment at Passover and to be liberated through the exodus. The "mercy seat" of Romans 3:25 is what Jesus means by his own death as a death "for them." Paul may be tying together the grand story of Israel in Romans as Jesus himself told it, but he does so without the warrant of Jesus' own words.

Why? *Because language is separate from the work of God even if it expresses that work of God truly. For the apostles no language enters the realm of finality.* The language games about atonement, from Jesus until today, anchor themselves more or less in the story of the Bible, but no one atonement story can ever achieve utter perfection. Every rhetoric of atonement is limited, and each one describes truths of the atonement, but no one rhetoric describes it all. The *deep reality* of atonement can only be brushed against, the way an artist paints a forest or a mountain. The artistic expression or the rhetoric provided are *iconic* in that they are designed to lead the person into the reality.

And they do.

THE STORY OF PAUL: IN THE
COURTROOM OF GOD

[Justification] is God's declaration that those who believe are in the right; their sins have been dealt with; they are God's true covenant people, God's renewed humanity.

—N. T. Wright[1]

If I may be so bold, the singular contribution of the Reformation doctrine of atonement and justification was that of double imputation. Justification is the courtroom declaration of God that an individual human is forgiven and in good standing with God. This declaration could occur, the Reformation thinkers argued, *because of God's imputing a human's sin to Christ and then imputing Christ's active obedience and righteousness to that human.* A consistent understanding of the Reformation's theory of justification is that it is bound up with double imputation.

I not only agree with double imputation, I up it. I think being "in Christ" involves multiple imputations: every thing we are is shuffled to Christ and all that Christ can offer is shuffled to us. It is that big. He became what we are so that we could become what he is, to summarize the early theologians (more of this in the next chapter).

If Jesus' story of atonement is Passover and liberation, one of the central stories of atonement that Paul tells is that of justification. This term "justification," however, has become contentious among theologians today because of the provocative suggestiveness of the New Perspective on Paul—roughly, the new understanding of Paul that flowed out of the rediscovery of the centrality and fecundity of Jewish sources (especially the Dead Sea Scrolls) and how that rediscovery reshaped what we think of Judaism at the time of Paul. Once again, roughly put, the notion that Jews sought to accumulate sufficient merit before God through good works in order to find salvation was put to the chase by a seminal study by E. P. Sanders, *Paul and Palestinian Judaism.* Since the publication of Sanders' work, there has been constant revision of how we perceive both Judaism at the time of Jesus and Paul and how their messages interact with that Judaism. Overall, since Judaism was not what we thought it was, neither was Christianity.[2]

The New Perspective on Paul

The New Perspective on Paul, which is a monolithic category foisted upon a diversity of viewpoints (and not always with accuracy), nearly all of which flow from the work of Ed Sanders, Jimmy Dunn, and Tom Wright (footnotes omitted), is asking us to reconsider what justification means. The New Perspective is both consistent with the Reformers' view of justification and simultaneously an attempt to take justification to a new level by making it more Jewish and Pauline (creating discontinuity with the Reformers). In other words, there is a meta-Reformation principle at work here: the New Perspective contends that many defenders of the Reformers' view of justification are defending Tradition even as the New Perspective seeks one more time to return to the Bible, in its historical context, to find what it originally said. In other words, the New Perspective is arguing for a new application of *sola scriptura* against sacred tradition.

Most important, though, the New Perspective thinks Paul is telling a bigger story of atonement than the Reformers thought Paul was telling. The New Perspective, in other words, gives new shape to the story of atonement. It might be easiest to suggest that the Reformation told the story of an individual, soteriological understanding of atonement and the New Perspective wants to tell an *individual, ecclesial, and soteriological* story of justification.

Justification in New Perspective

Let me summarize how I understand God's "right-making" or "justification," and I shall do so by drawing on Tom Wright's essay "The Shape of Justification."

A Future Forensic Decision Brought into Effect Now

First, God's right-making and justification is a forensic, or legal, image. God is the judge; *on the Final Day* God will judge all and declare some guilty and some righteous or acquitted (so Calvin) or vindicated (so Rom. 2:1–3:20). Those who find favor with God on that day are the covenanted family of God (Rom. 4). By claiming that those in Christ are already justified, Paul is declaring that the future judgment of God is reaching into time now—final eschatology is in the process of realization now.

Jesus and Then Those "in Christ" Are Declared in the Right

Second, Jesus' life, death, and resurrection incarnate God's covenant plan for Israel, so that Jesus is the second Adam (e.g., Rom. 5:12-21), the second Israel, and most especially the Son of God (1:3-6). Jesus' resurrection, therefore, is the decisive act in which God declares that Jesus is in the right (4:25).

The Presence of the Future

Third, those who are "in Christ" now already participate in that Final Day justification because they are "in Christ," who has been raised to the right hand of the Father (4:13-25; 5:1-11). Shot through and through Paul's understanding of present justification is eschatology: the justified community of faith is living now in light of a future finality through union with Christ.

Both Jews and Gentiles

Fourth, the family of God in the present is comprised of *both Jews and Gentiles* who believe in the God who raised Jesus from the dead. God originally promised a universal family (Gen. 12; cf. Gal. 3:1-14, 28), and the "justified" family "in Christ" is the fulfillment of that promise and the anticipation of its future perfection. Persons, whether Jew or Gentile, are plunged into this universal family of God through faith in Jesus Christ and through baptism that embodies that faith as a co-death and co-resurrection, which leads to the Spirit of adoption (Rom. 6–8).

Surely the element of freshness here is that justification is declared on behalf of those who have "faith" rather than to those who have "works of the law." Since the work of grace in Jesus' death and resurrection creates a universal ecclesial body, these works have got to go. They threaten *both* faith and the universal nature of the body of Christ. Here again is an ecclesial emphasis in God's "right-making."

Cosmic Justification

Fifth, God's "right-making" is, to one degree or another, an aspect of making the whole world right. That is, it is an aspect of Israel (through the Messiah) becoming a blessing to the whole world (Gen. 12:3). In fact, justification is an aspect of the redemption of the cosmos. So Romans 8:21-22: "the creation itself will be set free from its bondage to decay and will obtain the freedom of the glory of the children of God. We know that the whole creation has been groaning in labor pains until now...." Any fair reading of this passage reveals also that cosmic redemption follows in the wake of Eikonic redemption. As C. S. Lewis once put it, "And there are strange, exciting hints in the Bible that when we are drawn in, a great many other things in Nature will begin to come right."[3] Justification, as I read New Perspective writers, is an aspect of cosmic redemption.

Definitions

Now, after summarizing Wright with some of my own additions, I quote Tom's definition of what we can call the story of justification:

> "Justification" is thus the *declaration* of God, the just judge, that someone is (a) in the right, that their sins are forgiven, and (b) a true member of the covenant family, the people belonging to Abraham.... [The term justification] doesn't describe *how* people *get in* to God's forgiven family; it *declares that they are in*.[4]

This view is not entirely consistent with the Reformers' theory of justification for, though Wright sees justification as God's declaration of acquittal (so Calvin), it does not emphasize (as did the Reformers) that justification is also about *how people get **into** the family of God: they first must be declared right*. But, the Reformed theologians today ask, how does one "get in"? Is it not by virtue of double imputation? Is not imputation central to a Reformed understanding of atonement and justification? It is not clear that some in the New Perspective believe, as did the Reformers, in double imputation.[5] But anyone who sees, as does Tom Wright, God's atoning work in the life, death, and resurrection of Jesus as the recapitulation of

Adam and Israel as the Son of God has more than enough grounds to see Jesus' righteousness as that which is imputed to the family of God, with their sins imputed to him. If union with Christ is given a fair hearing, imputation follows. This is how one must read 1 Corinthians 1:30—Christ is *our* righteousness—and also 2 Corinthians 5:21: "For our sake he made him to be sin who knew no sin, so that in him we might become the righteousness of God." I hasten to add, however, that one *need not* read these texts as double imputation (as it is read in the Reformers' stricter categories), nor need one believe in double imputation in order to make sense of Paul's language. Frankly, I think it makes sense of the texts we have, but that Paul himself falls short of saying it just like that should give even the staunchest of Protestants reason to take a gulp (of intellectual humility).

Someone who puts these ideas into one dense formula is Michael Bird. Here is his definition of justification as he wends his way through the thickets of Reformed and New Perspective interaction:

> Justification is forensic (it refers to status not moral state), eschatological (the verdict of judgment day is declared in the present), covenantal (Jews and Gentiles belong in one fellowship table), and is effective (sanctification cannot be subsumed under justification but neither can they be completely separated).[6]

Several issues need to be explored in light of this *new understanding* of justification. In particular, justification in this new view is both corporate and individual; it is relational as well as judicial; it flows from the "in Christ" theme, giving a less-than-totally-legal context; and therefore, finally, it is not just a declaration but also an actual "right-making" in the here and now. I will look at each of these aspects, and each of them expresses what an emerging theology of atonement is all about. They also provide a reason why I call this book *A **Community** Called Atonement*.

Justification: Beyond Individualism

The Reformers' view of justification had two weaknesses: the entire work of God was swallowed by a radical individualism and the Reformed notion of justification became too judicial in substance. Neither of these points is wrong, of course; each, however, led to biblical imbalance. What the New Perspective is groping for is the fullness of what the apostle Paul has in mind.

Another major player in the New Perspective, Jimmy Dunn, says it best, and in saying it as he does he pits the New Perspective against the individualization of justification in Reformed thinking:

> The Christian doctrine of justification by faith begins as Paul's protest not as an individual sinner against a Jewish legalism, but as Paul's protest on behalf of Gentiles against Jewish exclusivism.[7]

The single most important passage in the history of the discussion of atonement is Romans 3:21-26. On its own, it can be shaped to say many things. Romans 1:18–3:20 tells us that *both Jews and Gentiles* are pressed into court to hear a guilty sentence read: "All, Jews and Gentiles, are found guilty of sin." But that verdict is not the final verdict. The work of God, his making things right in Christ, is a work in which God "declares in the right" *both Jews and Gentiles* by the same means: by faith. Justification, then, is about creating a society in which all are embraced by God's grace in Christ, through the Spirit, by faith.

Justification: Beyond Judicialization

A second problem in the Reformed understanding of justification concerns an over-judicialization of atonement imagery. A "modified" Reformed thinker like Hans Boersma has stated this tendency in Reformed thinking well:

> To affirm a juridical element in the atonement does not mean, however, that we should *reduce* the atonement to juridical elements, to law court scenes, or to notions of personal forgiveness of sins. When I speak about the juridicizing of the atonement, I have in mind a form of reductionism that limits the divine-human relationship to judicial categories, and that views the cross solely in terms of laws, infractions, judicial pronouncements, forgiveness, and punishments.[8]

And British Baptist theologian Paul Fiddes puts it like this:

> Some preaching thus reduces the event of the cross to a factor in an equation, formulated by a divine mathematician; a death is needed to balance the cosmic sum, and a death is provided.

When the death of Jesus is presented as a legal device for satisfying a divine justice which has been affronted by human sin, this can easily reduce the doctrine of atonement to a mere formula.

[Justification] is not an impersonal notice of acquittal which could be issued long ago and left lying around for us to pick up in due time, but a healing of relationship that must involve us *now* as the ones who are estranged.[9]

What the New Perspective brings to the table is that justification needs to be given a more relational understanding (without eliminating the important judicial context). It asks us to get out of the tendency to reduce justification to the judicial and to expand justification into its rightful Hebraic, relational context.

Justification must be understood as an expression of God's gracious love and gracious desire to be in union with God's people. As my own professor, Jimmy Dunn, wrote so eloquently about this Lutheran discovery:

The insight granted to Luther has remained at the heart of Protestant Christian thought. 'Justification by faith' is a sharp sword which punctures all inflated thoughts of self-importance. It is a sharp knife which cuts away all reliance on human effort, on human cleverness. It is a sharp spade which undermines any attempt to build our own protective barriers or control our own destiny. It cuts through all human pretence, all human self-assurance, all human boasting. God accepts not the important, or the activist, or the clever, or the powerful as such. It is the *sinner* he accepts. That is an insight which has been applied over and over again in Christian critique of false religiosity and political systems. It is an insight which must never be lost from the gospel....
There is more to it, of course.[10]

Here we have it: justification concerns being restored in a relationship with God (and others, as our previous section showed) by the sheer goodness of God's bountiful grace.

Justification: Beyond Reductionism

This emphasis on relationship extends into seeing the proper context for justification in the story of Paul. God's making people right is itself part of a larger network of God's redemptive work and it is reductionistic not to connect justification to union with Christ. The ground for justification, as Reformed scholar D. A. Carson argues, is being "in Christ."[11] Thus, *incorporation* is the foundation for justification. This is why Tom Wright's second point above is so central to any adequate theory of justification or atonement: it all comes down to one thing—being incorporated into Christ, which showers the one so incorporated with all the blessings expected in God's covenant.

Notice the order of Paul's words from this text: God "is the source of your life in Christ Jesus, who [Christ] became for us [1] wisdom from God, and [2] righteousness and [3] sanctification and [4] redemption" (1 Cor. 1:30). That is: God acted to join us to Christ, and by being "in" Christ we obtain the blessings of wisdom, righteousness [justification], sanctification, and redemption. The order: union with Christ (relational incorporation) entails righteousness.

Justification: Beyond a Verdict

What is the *telic* force of justification? What happens to the person? Are they simply declared forgiven in a courtroom (in God's presence) or are they changed? We need to remind ourselves of something about some words and their history of usage. "Justification" is a gray-bearded term that is religious; "justice" is a modern term that is social; "righteous" and "righteousness" are religious and moral terms. These terms belong together in Greek and in Hebrew. To be righteous, or to be justified, is to heal the comprehensive "crackedness" of Eikons so that they become "right" in their relation with God, with self, with others (especially the poor and powerless), and the world.

The Reformation asked us to see "justification," God's "declaration," as a *forensic* image and to keep it there. It is accurate to give the term a forensic emphasis, but it was *impossible* for a first-century Jew to say "righteous/ness," deriving as it does from the deeply meaningful Hebrew word *tsedeq*, without also thinking of three other objects: God, Torah, and Israel. Justification, put differently, has the creative power to make anew because when God declares one "righteous," righteousness really happens.

God is righteous. That is the rock-bottom, ontological reality according to the Bible. And when the Bible says that God is righteous, there are three ideas at work: God's attribute of being right or morally perfect, God's faithfulness to his covenant promises (e.g., Ps. 31:1), and God's acts of bringing the world into a rectified condition. In other words, God, who is righteous and who will honor his word, acts to make things right; God, who is righteous, acts in a creative, saving, judging manner. Thus, Psalm 71:15-16:

> My mouth will tell of your *righteous acts*,
>   of your deeds of *salvation* all day long,
>   though their number is past my knowledge.
> I will come praising the *mighty deeds* of the Lord GOD,
>   I will praise your *righteousness*, yours alone. (emphasis added)

To be "righteous" in Israel was to observe the Torah—this can't be disputed. But righteousness is not just observance of the Torah by random Israelites in a personal relationship with God. It also involved both *moral rectitude* (hence, the call to be "just" or "righteous" or to have "righteousness"—as in, say, Matt. 5:17-20) and *ecclesial rectitude* (the establishment of a society in which God's will is done) as expressive of right relations. Justification does not stop with a verdict: its telic force and intent is to create a community wherein justice (or righteousness) is embodied in relations and behaviors. This is the only way to read Romans 6:7: "For whoever has died is freed [lit., *justified*] from sin." This verse is not simply about the verdict of forgiveness, but emerges in a context of the "old self" being "crucified with him [Christ]" so that "we might no longer be enslaved to sin" (6:6). What Paul has in mind is the *moral impact* of the forensic declaration: those "in Christ" are transformed. As Doug Moo puts it: we are "set free from [the power] of sin."[12]

To be righteous in the first century was to be in a community dedicated to *Torah*, to the will of God. Jeremiah 31:31-33 sketches an image in which some day, some way, God will restore his people *Israel* so that they become righteous—and that means that they will become a society in which the will of God is done. Righteousness always involves the "Other" and "others"; it is impossible to speak of righteousness in a purely individual sense. Righteousness is the characteristic of a community that does what God wants in relation to one another. The forensically declared status of righteousness with God produces the right relation with God and a right relation with God produces a right relation with others.[13]

A Story with Many Stories

There is a certain pristine ruggedness about each of the metaphors used for atonement. On their own they speak; theologians combine and coalesce them into a synthetic harmony that, while clever at the level of propositions and articulations and logic, does not express the grandeur that each story has on its own. However, these various stories of atonement, whether we look to Jesus and Passover or to Paul and justification (and he himself had other stories), or whether we look to the early fathers or to the Reformers, *compete with one another*. They compete not by fighting with the others in order to gain mastery but by being language games that are not easily assimilated to one another. Each club in the bag performs its own task. It is impossible to swing two clubs at once. Before I propose a bag into which all the clubs fit, I want to sketch the earliest "bag" designed to carry the clubs, the atonement theory of Irenaeus and Athanasius.

C H A P T E R
T H I R T E E N

THE STORY OF EARLY THEOLOGIANS: IRENAEUS AND ATHANASIUS

He has therefore, in His work of recapitulation, summed up all things . . . in order that, as our species went down to death through a vanquished man, so we may ascend to life again through a victorious one.

—Irenaeus[1]

The church decided early on that the stories that are found in the Bible to express atonement—stories as diverse as covenant and Passover and promise and exodus and tabernacle and temple and sacrifice and exile/return and new covenant and justification and redemption and reconciliation and heavenly temple—could be both expanded and reshaped. Within a generation or two of the apostles, a new rhetoric was sought, a rhetoric that engaged the Bible and simultaneously expressed the currents of the day. I am thinking especially of the story of atonement found in Irenaeus and Athanasius.

Perhaps the first thing that began to happen among these early theologians was the *attempt to put the story into a meaningful and new shape.* They wrote what can only be called an emerging, *living theology.* Yes, it was biblical; yes, it was also traditional. But, at the same time, it was swallowed into a new living and breathing whole. That new whole partook of philosophical currents, contemporary culture, personal style, apologetical boundary-marking, and pastoral-missional direction. It would have its day, and the next generation of theologians would have their day, too. That, lest we forget, is what theology has always been about.

Recapitulation

Irenaeus and Athanasius usually are assigned to a theory of the atonement called *recapitulation*. In many ways these two theologians—and there were others around them—set the tone for all theories of atonement that followed. Historians of theology will perhaps correct my suggestion, but it seems to me that the thread of recapitulation can be found at each major moment in the unfolding history of atonement theories.

In its broad sense, the story of recapitulation (Greek *anakephalaiosis*, or "bringing to a head") teaches that Jesus "recapitulated" Adam's life, Israel's life, and the life of every one of us—male and female, Western and Eastern, Southern and Northern. Of course, neither Irenaeus nor Athanasius cared about us—and many of us have returned the favor by never reading a word of theirs or about them! We might observe that their word *anakephalaiosis* was used by the apostle Paul for love that, according to Romans 13:9, *sums up*, or brings into complete unity, all the commandments. This illustrates what the early theologians had in mind: as love recapitulates, or brings into fullness, all commandments, so Christ recapitulates all of humanity. Recapitulation was, then, the name of the bag in which they carried their theological clubs.

There are two dimensions to the story of recapitulation. First, Christ recapitulates in an *exclusive* sense. He alone stands in our place—later to be called "substitution"—and does what we cannot do. He lives for us and instead of us. And, second, Christ recapitulates in an *inclusive* sense. He represents us as we are summoned to participate in his work by being "in him." We are, in yet another term, "incorporated" into *his* actions. We don't do what he does alongside him; we join in what he does.

The genius of what these theologians were working out was that Jesus' incarnate life and death and resurrection, along with his descent into hell and his exaltation, were *done for us* and they *included us* so that our life is lived in Christ. As Irenaeus puts it so clearly in the preface to the fifth book of *Against Heresies*: "but following the only true and stedfast Teacher, the Word of God, our Lord Jesus Christ, who did, through His transcendent love, become what we are, that He might bring us to be even what He is Himself." And Athanasius, whose work stands behind all of Eastern Orthodoxy and Christian orthodoxy, said it like this: "For He was made man that we might be made God."[2]

Such a story of atonement is profoundly biblical. Its biblical roots are in the representative character of Moses and David, and even more in the

Son of Man of Daniel 7 or in the Servant of Isaiah. Matthew and Luke clearly present the temptations of Jesus as the reliving of Israel's wanderings in the wilderness so that Jesus is a second Israel (Matt. 4:1-11; Luke 4:1-13), and the apostle Paul sketches the notion that Jesus is the second Adam (Rom. 5:12-21), and the writer of Hebrews clearly says that Jesus had to be made like us in every way so that he, as the greatest of all high priests, could ransom us from our condition (Heb. 2:14-18). What all of these suggest for atonement is that Jesus became all that we are—he *absolutely identified himself* with the fullness of humans—so that he might lead us to God.

Death and Life

We best enter the story of atonement found in Irenaeus and Athanasius when we begin with what they saw as the central problem: *death* (and corruption and mortality). And if the central problem is death, then the work of God brings *life* (and incorruption and immortality). Paul, in Romans, wrote as a "thanatologist" or at least a mortician—one who studied and dealt with death; this is why Paul is also focused constantly on death-in-Adam and life-in-Christ (cf. Rom. 6–8).

Athanasius, too, was obsessed with death as the human condition, and he contends that Jesus' identification with us becomes substitutionary in his dying for us:

> For this cause, then, *death* having gained upon men, and *corruption* abiding upon them, the race of man was *perishing*; the rational man made in God's image was *disappearing*, and the handiwork of God was in process of *dissolution*.[3] (emphasis added)

> He took pity on our race, and had mercy on our *infirmity*, and condescended to our *corruption* ... [and] gave [His body] over to *death in the stead of all* ... [that] He might turn them again toward incorruption, and quicken them from *death* by the appropriation of His body and by the grace of the Resurrection, banishing *death* from them like straw from the fire.[4] (emphasis added)

Irenaeus says this of the entire impact of Jesus Christ: "God recapitulated in Himself the ancient formation of man, that He might kill sin, deprive death of its power, and vivify man."[5] This is the story of death being swallowed up into life.

Eastern theology develops this conviction (of death being transformed through Christ's death and resurrection) into a concept called *theopoesis* (also *theosis*), sometimes translated "divinization" or "deification." The Eastern theologians do not contend that in eternity humans will be absorbed into the being of God, as in some forms of pantheism, but that humans will remain distinct, integral human personalities. But, still, they will partake (as 2 Peter 1 says) in God's very incorruptible life, and they will—and this is the whole point of salvation—*be drawn into the life of God by partaking of his eternal life*. Salvation is being drawn into the life of God; it is *theopoesis*. While I'm aware that many today get nervous when they hear a term like "divinization," I am fully persuaded that this rich Christian term needs to be cherished more.

A major text used to support this theory is John 10:34-35 and, along with that text, its Old Testament grounding, Psalm 82:6-7:

John 10:34-35:
Jesus answered, "Is it not written in your law, 'I said, you are gods'? If those to whom the word of God came were called 'gods'—and the scripture cannot be annulled—"

Psalm 82:6-7:
I say, "You are gods,
    children of the Most High, all of you;
nevertheless, you shall die like mortals,
    and fall like any prince."

These two texts litter the writings of the early theologians, but the focus of the verses, as Carl Mosser makes clear in his exacting study that shows that their early exegesis was thoroughly Jewish, is not on becoming *divine* but on becoming *sons of God*.[6] Hence, another popular text was, as quoted above, Galatians 4:4-6: God sent his Son so that we might become God's children.

To sum up, then, this line of thinking was that the eternal focal point of our destiny is to put death behind us so that we can be elevated into the very presence of God, partaking of God's very own *life* as his distinct children, and that redemptive process is now at work in the people of God.

Incarnation

A second feature of this early story of atonement is that it rests heavily (some would say too heavily) on the *incarnation*. Here is one of my all-time favorite lines from a theologian, this one from Irenaeus:

> For it was incumbent upon the Mediator between God and men, by His relationship to both, *to bring both to friendship and concord*, and present man to God, while He revealed God to man.... For it behooved Him who was to destroy sin, and redeem man under the power of death, *that He should Himself be made that very same thing which he was, that is, man*; who had been drawn by sin into bondage, but was held by death, so that sin should be destroyed by man, and man should go forth from death.[7] (emphasis added)

Some Eastern theologians even contend that it is the incarnation that saves, but a more even-keeled survey of the writings of these theologians suggests that it is not the incarnation *per se* that redeems. No, redemption occurs both through *who* the incarnate Son was and what the incarnate Son *did*. He went to the cross to die for humans (thereby partaking in corruption "in our stead") so that he could bring incorruption to humans. And here it all comes together for Irenaeus: "God *recapitulated* in Himself the ancient formation of man, that He might kill sin, deprive death of its power, and vivify man" (emphasis added).

Victory

Enter now another central element of this story of atonement: the *victory* or the *liberation* that comes from being ransomed. Some prefer to describe the atonement theory of the Eastern theologians as the ransom theory, but focusing on that term leads to the extreme form of ransom theory found later in homiletical form, especially in Gregory of Nyssa— namely, that God tricked the devil into grasping for Jesus and then the resurrection permitted the Son to escape from the devil's clutches. I prefer to approach the early theologians through recapitulation, and see the ransom element coming to fruition in victory so that recapitulation becomes what is now called a *Christus Victor* theory. Irenaeus anticipated extremes in ransom theology, and called attention to them by saying that God's methods were

> by means of *persuasion*, as became a God of counsel, who *does not use violent means* to obtain what He desires.

And here is what the atonement brings:

> Since the Lord thus has redeemed us through His own blood, giving His soul for our souls, and His flesh for our flesh, and has also poured out the

Spirit of the Father *for the union and communion of God and man, imparting indeed God to men by means of the Spirit, and, on the other hand, attaching man to God by His own incarnation, and bestowing upon us at His coming immortality durably and truly, by means of communion with God....* [8] (emphasis added)

This, then, is the earliest post-biblical Christian story of atonement: human sin defaces the Eikon of God, a favorite image of early theologians, and sinks humans into corruption and death. But God, joining together humans and God in the incarnate Word, becomes what we are so that we might become what he is—so vanquishing death and drawing us into the very life and presence of God. As Georges Florovsky has it, "In the Incarnation the Word assumes the first-formed human nature, created 'in the image of God,' and thereby the image of God is again re-established."[9] We have here an atonement theory that begins with union with Christ, finds expression in substitutionary atonement, and continues into the focus of union with God.

The Paschal Homily

It is not possible to be fair to the early Eastern theologians without bringing in John Chrysostom's famous Paschal homily. This famous sermon plays the distinctive notes of the earliest Christian theory of atonement. In addition, we find another element of those beliefs, namely the harrowing of hell in Christ's descent. Chrysostom's sermon is read every Easter in Orthodox worship to this day. Here are the final two paragraphs:

He has destroyed death by undergoing death.
He has despoiled hell by descending into hell.
He vexed it even as it tasted of His flesh.
Isaiah foretold this when he cried:
Hell was filled with bitterness when it met Thee face to face
    below;
    filled with bitterness, for it was brought to nothing;
    filled with bitterness, for it was mocked;
    filled with bitterness, for it was overthrown;
    filled with bitterness, for it was put in chains.
Hell received a body, and encountered God. It received earth, and
    confronted heaven.
O death, where is your sting?
O hell, where is your victory?

Christ is risen! And you, o death, are annihilated!
Christ is risen! And the evil ones are cast down!
Christ is risen! And the angels rejoice!
Christ is risen! And life is liberated!
Christ is risen! And the tomb is emptied of its dead;
for Christ having risen from the dead,
is become the first-fruits of those who have fallen asleep.

To Him be Glory and Power, now and forever, and from all ages to
all ages. Amen![10]

Mystery

Now to summarize. The emphasis here is on *death* and *life*. The solution to the problem of death is the incarnate Word's life, death, and resurrection, but with clear emphasis on the incarnation's capacity to join divine nature with human nature in order to lead us to God and be drawn into his very life. Such a theory draws heavily, for starters, on Philippians 2:6-11, with its emphasis on incarnation, *kenosis*, and exaltation; it draws even more directly on the incarnational notes of John 1:1-14, and it finds all of this in the cosmic myth of God versus Satan that is retold in the form of a New Exodus. The central place of redemption in this perspective is the Eucharist, for here the Eikon partakes of union with God.

We have now examined several issues in our attempt to put together a model of the atonement. We have looked at metaphor, we have looked at the major moments of atonement, and we have observed that each person tells the atonement story in a singular image. We are bound, obviously, to follow their lead. Any theologian or preacher or Christian who attempts in any way to explain the gospel is bound to tell that gospel story in the form of an atonement theory. Which one, we might ask, best tells the story today? Which one is comprehensive enough to suggest that all the models are included? I shall now attempt to describe a bag that I think can hold all the clubs.

CHAPTER
FOURTEEN

WHICH IS THE FAIREST OF THEM ALL?

The One who was offended bears the burden of the offense.
—Miroslav Volf[1]

Here's my proposal for a bag that can hold all the metaphorical clubs: I suggest that we think of atonement as *identification for incorporation.* I take Hebrews 2:14-18 to be thematic of the entire scope of the atonement:

> Since, therefore, the children share flesh and blood, he himself likewise *shared the same things,* so that *through death* he might *destroy the one who has the power of death,* that is, the devil, and *free those who all their lives were held in slavery by the fear of death.* For it is clear that he did not come to help angels, but the descendants of Abraham. Therefore *he had to become like his brothers and sisters in every respect, so that he might be a merciful and faithful high priest in the service of God, to make a sacrifice of atonement for the sins of the people.* Because *he himself was tested* by what he suffered, he is *able to help* those who are being tested. (emphasis added)

Jesus *identifies* with humans: "he had to become like his brothers and sisters." Jesus *incorporates* humans in his destruction of death and the devil and liberates those held captive by being a faithful high priest for them (representing them before God as priests do). Jesus identifies and makes possible incorporation because he "shared flesh and blood" and because he became a "sacrifice of atonement" (*eis to hilaskesthai*) for the sins of humans. Which means that Jesus died *for them, with them, and instead of them*: their death became his so that his life might become theirs.

His act of atonement has a dual focus in light of the enormity of the problem with cracked Eikons: identification in order to remove sins *and* victory in order to liberate those who are incorporated into him so that they can form the new community where God's will is realized. In this scoping out of atonement, we find its centrality in relationship: in being connected to Christ, in being in union with Christ, in being "in" Christ. He *identifies* with us all the way down to death in order that we might be *incorporated* into him. To be incorporated "in Christ" is not only a personal relationship with Jesus Christ but also a personal relationship with his people.

Identification

Identification with us grounds atonement. Jesus, the Son of God, is God incarnate who *identifies with us*. He became what we are, Athanasius said. He became fully human yet was without sin, the writer of Hebrews says in 4:15. The Gospel of John has an opening with no parallel in the entire Bible, apart perhaps from Genesis 1—and the focus of that opening finds its fulfillment in 1:14: "And the Word *became flesh and lived among us*, and we have seen his glory, the glory as of a father's only son, full of grace and truth" (emphasis added). Incarnation propels atonement for the purpose of identification.

The Eastern church's emphasis, along with atonement's further centrality in Anselm, the Reformers, and Anglican thought, gets it right: atonement requires that God becomes human. Without engaging the endless debates about persons and natures and hypostases, it can be said that one thing the incarnation tells us is that Jesus Christ *identifies with us* in our human condition, yet without sin.

Words other than "identification" work here, too—like sympathy or participation or incarnation. Whichever term we use, what we have in the Christian perspective is that God knows what we go through, and not just as an omniscient God who happens to know us along with everything else, but as one who *knows* us by participating in our condition.[2] Incarnation teaches that God has identified with us. He is with us in our living and our dying, in our joys and our sorrows, in our good days and our bad days. Most important, God has entered (as the German theologian Jürgen Moltmann has so ably shown over and over) into our sin and its sufferings. In the moment of Jesus' full entry into sin on our behalf, God suffered. In what seems to be the total absence of God we learn the mystery of God's inescapable presence.

For Incorporation

Identification has purpose: incorporation.

God sends the Son into this world, the Fourth Gospel tells us, to set in motion the earthly *missio Dei*, the mission of God to bring the world to its consummation, to restore cracked Eikons, to heal humans in all four relational directions. Cracked Eikons are set on the path of restoration by union with Christ, by being incorporated into Christ, by believing, receiving, eating, drinking, following, and obeying Jesus, the Son of God who is the second Adam.

Everything good happens to the Christian by virtue of union with Christ. Nothing makes this clearer than the "in Christ" theme of Paul's letters. Here are some sterling New Testament examples of this language, and their number could be multiplied:

Redemption is in Christ: "through the redemption that is in Christ Jesus" (Rom. 3:24)

Death and life in Christ: "So you also must consider yourselves dead to sin and alive to God in Christ Jesus" (Rom. 6:11; see 1 Cor. 15:22)

God's love in Christ: nothing "will be able to separate us from the love of God in Christ Jesus" (Rom. 8:39)

Unity in Christ: "we are one body in Christ" (Rom. 12:5)

Ministry in Christ: "Greet Urbanus, our co-worker in Christ" (Rom. 16:9; see 1 Cor. 4:15)

Sanctified in Christ: "to those who are sanctified in Christ Jesus" (1 Cor. 1:2)

New creation in Christ: "So if anyone is in Christ, there is a new creation" (2 Cor. 5:17)

Reconciliation of the world in Christ: "in Christ God was reconciling the world to himself" (2 Cor. 5:19)

Freedom in Christ: "to spy on the freedom we have in Christ Jesus" (Gal. 2:4)

Justification in Christ: "to be justified in Christ" (Gal. 2:17)

Universal redemption in Christ: "There is no longer Jew or Greek, there is no longer slave or free, there is no longer male and female; for all of you are one in Christ Jesus" (Gal. 3:28)

Blessings in Christ: "who has blessed us in Christ with every spiritual blessing" (Eph. 1:3)

Jesus identifies with us and we gain access to everything he is by being incorporated into him, by entering into this "in Christ" realm. *Every theory of the atonement emerges from this central, life-giving identification for incorporation.* Atonement is what happens to a human being who is united with Christ. Union with Christ, in other words, is the foundation of atonement, and those who are so in union form the new community where cracked Eikons can be restored to God, self, others, and the world.

I am using "identification for incorporation" as a variant on the older recapitulation theory, but I do so not because I think recapitulation is flawed but because I think it too is in need of an expansive set of terms that tells the whole story of atonement. It is worth our while now to explore how *identification for incorporation* embraces all the models of atonement.

Getting Our Metaphors in the Bag

Recapitulation

I begin with what I think is probably the oldest theory after the apostolic age. If we take the *recapitulation* theory of those like Irenaeus up through Athanasius, we are hearing the central core of what I am calling identification for incorporation: Jesus became what we are so that we could become what he is. Those early fathers, of course, explained the atoning work of God as more than recapitulation and sometimes used expressions that sound like satisfaction or substitution, but since this theory is sometimes understood as the oldest and is given a distinctive, on-its-own status, it needs to be seen as the core of what I am saying with my "identification for incorporation."

Ransom/Christus Victor

The *ransom* theory, or what Aulén and others sometimes call the *Christus Victor* or classical theory of atonement, focuses on a mechanism within the identification for incorporation theme. Jesus' identification was to the point of death, of being captured, as it were, by sin and death and the devil, and his powerful resurrection broke the chains of this captivity and set us free. That is, he identified with us "all the way down" (as postmodernists might say) and rescued us, liberated us, and set us free. But this liberation from sin, death, and devil is by way of being *incorporated into Christ.* We somehow have to become attached to Christ for the ransom to occur.

Satisfaction

The *satisfaction* theory, which is constantly being deconstructed today by those who want to tie it into the knots of a medieval justice system, fits inside our identification for incorporation theory. That is, Jesus' identification with us is an identification with our sinful, guilty, God-dishonoring condition—what I call the cracked Eikon—and this, so we must argue if we want to be biblical and theological, is in some sense a satisfaction of what God needs for God to be given his proper glory.

The legal element of this theory can be easily overcooked, and the theory itself often has been burnt on such theorizing. But at some level we must admit that Jesus' identification with us "all the way down" is an identification with our sinful condition and the just judgment we know as fair in God's assessment of what we have done to mess up the Eikon. And, along with Anselm, I think that the notion that Jesus is the God-Man on our behalf fits perfectly into what I am calling "identification." That Jesus "identifies" with us—that is, becomes one of us—is what Anselm saw as necessary in order to take up our case before God. I don't think the satisfaction theory is sufficiently robust to carry the day: it lacks an emphasis on what I am calling incorporation, it becomes too legal and judicial and therefore non-relational—the criticisms have all been marched out by others. My point is that identification for incorporation carries within it an element of satisfaction.

Substitution

A central term in atonement theory is *substitution*, which conveys the idea that Jesus Christ did something for us that we could not do for ourselves—that he did something *instead of us*. Identification with us *can only lead* to incorporation if we surrender our minds to the thoroughly biblical and Christian notion that Jesus does something (make that some things) for us *that we could not do ourselves*. He died *instead of* us and for our sins so that we could be raised with him to new life. For some good reasons and then some bad reasons added for good measure, some today steer clear of the term "substitution." My contention is that the ancient Israelite sacrificial system, with its intricate sense of sin and dispersal of sin on Yom Kippur (see Lev. 16; 23:26-32; Num. 29:7-11), makes most sense if the sending of the live goat into the wilderness is explained as a substitution—represented both in the laying on of hands and in the transfer of the sins onto the head of the goat. The goat is to bear the sins away to where the wild things are.

Debates today make "substitution" a politically heavy term, but I think 2 Corinthians 5:21 is a clear case of substitution: "For our sake he made him to be sin who knew no sin, so that in him we might become the righteousness of God." Jesus Christ did not know sin. He was innocent; he "was made" (Greek *epoiesen*) "sin" because we are sinful; he was made something he was not to be what we are; and he was made this so that we could be released from our condition and made what he is: "the righteousness of God." If there is a better word than "substitution" for this, then I'd use it. I do think we could (but need not) use another term, and I'll turn to that now.

Representation

One reason many are nervous about "substitution" is that it is not complete enough as a metaphor, and I agree with this: substitution is an element of what I am calling identification. Instead of substitution, many prefer the term *representation*. My own theory is that we ought to use the term representation more, for it is true that Jesus "represents" us the way a priest represents the people before God. The notion of representation is found in the king of Israel, in the priestly function, in the Son of Man, and in the servant of Isaiah, and it jumps off the page in the New Testament teaching of Jesus as being second Israel and second Adam. Representation is also important for the language game of the book of Hebrews to work.

But here again, representation is also not enough. This is why in my book *Jesus and His Death* I sought to explain the New Testament teaching through the term representation in two ways: there is an *inclusive* representation and an *exclusive* representation. We both die and rise *with* Christ (inclusive representation) and he dies and is raised *instead of us* but *for our benefit by incorporation* (exclusive representation). So, for my own use of language, I see exclusive representation to be synonymous with substitution.

The term *identification* involves both inclusive and exclusive representation: Jesus has completely identified with us so far "all the way down" that his excess of dying in our place, instead of us, and being raised in our place, instead of us, overcomes what humans deserve but do not suffer. He identifies with us completely in order to lift us from our condition, to restore cracked Eikons, by incorporating us into himself.

Penal Substitution

This brings us to *penal* substitution. Does the New Testament teach this? By all means, but when overly judicialized or reified, penal substitution distorts the fullness of the atonement. If we begin with identification for incorporation, with Christ's union with us and our union with him, we arrive at this very clear condition: *he becomes what we are so that we can become what he is.* What "we are" is clear: we are created as Eikons, we become cracked Eikons who are dying, and we are destined (by incorporation) to become Christ-like Eikons. It is his identification with cracked Eikons that grants fresh light on penal substitution. If we approach this idea through our union with Christ, the major problems vanish into bad uses of metaphors.

What, after all, is the punishment the Bible speaks of? It can all be summed up in one word: *death*. The consequence of eating from the forbidden tree is "lest you die." The serpent's counterclaim is that Adam and Eve will not die. The apostle Paul is a mortician: he is obsessed with and focused on *death*. The book of Romans has the term "death" (Greek *thanatos*) no fewer than twenty-two times, and it is especially prominent in chapters 5–8 where Paul unfolds his gospel and his understanding of what Christ has done on our behalf.

I think it is all clear from one verse, Romans 5:17: "If, because of the one man's trespass, *death* exercised dominion through that one, much more surely will those who receive the abundance of grace and the free gift of righteousness exercise dominion in *life* through the one man, Jesus Christ" (emphasis added). Here it is for Paul: Adam sins and the divine punishment (wrath) for sin brings death; Jesus obeys and brings life. He *identifies with us, all the way down into death (so Phil. 2:5-11), so that we can be incorporated into him and find life—both here and now and then and there.*

Does the Bible teach that Jesus suffered death on our part? Often.

So I conclude that the Bible does teach penal substitution: Jesus identified with us so far "all the way down" that he died our death, so that we, being incorporated into him, might partake in his glorious, life-giving resurrection to new life. He died instead of us (substitution); he died a death that was the consequence of sin (penal). But, here again, this is not enough; it is just not enough to express atonement through the category of penal substitution.

If we limit atonement to this category, we have an atonement that is nothing more than an important theodicy: it explains *how* God can eliminate sin justly, but it only explains the wrath-to-death problem, and that is not all there is to atonement.

What about Abelard?

There is one more theory, and some debate whether it is really an atonement metaphor at all. Abelard taught that Jesus' death was the supreme demonstration of the love of God that generates, in itself, regenerative love in our hearts so that we take up the cross and live a life of service to others. Now the popular understanding of Abelard is that Jesus is merely an example. That is not fair to Abelard, as scholars (like Paul Fiddes and Peter Schmiechen) have made clear. But, still, if the death of Christ is no more than an act of willing sacrifice on the part of Jesus, then we will be hard pressed to discover it to be an atoning act because, while it might change a life, it does not rid that person of sin. It becomes merely an exemplary act. However one looks at Abelard, he's right in this: Jesus' identification with us "all the way down" extends at least to a sacrificial death that, in and of itself, can generate in the beholder an awakening of love. It is true: the cross is a wondrous example of how far we can be challenged to go for the kingdom of God.

I rest my case here: what we are most in need of today is not a continuance of the atonement wars for a privileged metaphor, but a vigorous discussion of the value of each of the metaphors so that each image is invited to the table. And I contend that *identification for incorporation* is such an invitation and that it, along with perhaps similarly comprehensive categories, can create a conversation on atonement that is inclusive of all the metaphors. Lest it be charged that I am simply turning the tide back a notch in arguing for one metaphor, I'm not. I'm arguing instead for an embracive category, one that includes each metaphor in a larger, rounded whole. We need to use all the clubs in our bag and we need a bag that can hold them all.

Let me try on another image. The magic of a violin is the capacity for the violinist to make each string work in harmony with the others to create the appropriate sound. If a violinist somehow managed to play only one string on the violin, the sound could never be complete. Some theories of atonement ask violinists either to pluck all but one string or to play gospel music as though only one string really mattered. I want to contend that we need each of the strings, and that we need to seek for a violinist with a bow that can stroke the strings so well that the potency of each string creates a harmonious composition that puts our hearts at rest.

At this point many discussions of atonement end. But there is more ground to cover. We are now ready to explore atonement not only as the act of God but, as is the case with all emerging theology, *as something we are invited to perform with God in this world*. Atonement is *praxis*.

PART FOUR

Atonement as Praxis: Who Does Atonement?

C H A P T E R
F I F T E E N

ATONEMENT AS MISSIONAL PRAXIS: FELLOWSHIP

Jesus' gospel includes the fact that the messianic reign has in fact begun and there is now a reconciled and reconciling community whose visible life is a powerful sign of the kingdom that has already begun and will someday arrive in its fullness.

—Ronald Sider[1]

I stand here on the threshold of a doorway that few enter: *atonement is something done not only by God for us but also something we do with God for others*. This door opens to those who are learning that atonement is also *praxis*. That we suggest that atonement is also praxis is not an attack on the view that atonement is something God does for us. Instead, it is the conviction that atonement is embodied in what God does for us in such a way that we are summoned to participate with God in his redemptive work.

If atonement is the healing of the cracked Eikon in all four directions, and if we are involved in helping one another to heal in those directions, then atonement has to be discussed from the angle of praxis. Atonement as missional praxis is full-orbed: humans participate with God in world redemption and in restoring cracked Eikons in all four directions, and that means that healing in each direction is a dimension of atonement.

Theme

The thematic verse for this emerging theology of atonement as praxis is 2 Corinthians 5:18-20:

All this is from God, who reconciled us to himself through Christ, and has *given us the ministry of reconciliation*; that is, in Christ God was reconciling the world to himself, not counting their trespasses against them, and *entrusting the message of reconciliation to us*. So we are *ambassadors for Christ, since God is making his appeal through us*; we entreat you on behalf of Christ, be reconciled to God. (emphasis added)

This section of *A Community Called Atonement* will take this theme seriously: that cracked Eikons in the process of restoration have been entrusted with the message of reconciliation, that cracked Eikons are "ambassadors"—personal representatives of God on earth—for Christ, and that God is working "through us" to implore others to be reconciled to God to begin the healing of the Eikon and the world.

In the rest of this book there is no attempt to be comprehensive or exhaustive about what a missional praxis of atonement looks like. At rock-bottom reality each community will work out its own praxis of atonement, and that praxis will have a different shape and orientation in each community. The central question of a missional praxis is this: "How can we help?" This central question springs from a desire to go out into the community rather than an overwhelming drive to have the community come to the local church. To be sure, there is a Christ-orientation in all Christian questions that are shaped by "How can we help?" but that question is not simply a medium to evangelize but a genuine question that knows that all forms of helping are framed by the redemptive purposes of God.

Once again the relational core of atonement comes to the fore. It is not uncommon today to hear that we "belong" before we "believe" or that all truth must become incarnate or that truth is relational. If atonement is multirelational healing toward God, self, others, and world, then we need to keep before us the central reality that atonement is first and foremost a "belonging to God, to self, to others and to the world." Atonement is relational healing in all directions. No one has made this more clear today than LeRon Shults: we are defined by and find meaning in relations.[2] Which means that the first step we take when we seek to understand atonement as praxis is the step of relationship called "fellowship."

But lest I be accused of something worse than heresy, let me make it clear up front: I do not believe humans atone for others and I do not believe humans can atone for themselves. Atonement is the work of God—in Christ, through the Spirit—but God has chosen to summon us to participate in *God's* work, even though we are cracked Eikons or, to use Paul's words, "clay jars" (2 Cor. 4:7).

Fellowship: The Community of Atonement

We can begin anywhere in the Bible on this theme. We could begin with the creation of the covenanted community of Abraham, with the Torah-shaped community of worship and purity of Moses, with the kingdom-shaped community of David and Solomon, with the prophetically shaped summons to a more just community, with the restored-kingdom community of Jesus, with the Spirit-inspired community of the early churches of the land of Israel, with the ecclesially shaped communities of faith formed in the Pauline mission, with the suffering-shaped communities established by Peter in Asia Minor, or with the love-centered communities envisioned by the apostle John. Wherever you go in the Bible, it is the same: the work of God is *to form a community* in which the will of God is done and through which one finds both union with God and communion with others for the good of others and the world.

I will take as an example of what fellowship for atonement was like in the NT the churches Peter established in Asia Minor, churches in many cases quite unlike what modern suburbanites know but not unlike what inner city and rural churches might intuitively grasp. His readers were socially disenfranchised, most likely because they were classed as "resident aliens" and "temporary residents" (1 Pet. 1:1; 2:11-12), and they were suffering because they were associated with Jesus (4:12-19). Peter steps into this context with a Spirit-directed message that mixes together his tradition with their context in an emerging theology of survival.

Starts with Trinity

I make two observations. First, this fellowship or community derives from the *perichoretic* community of God. Peter writes to a set of churches in the Diaspora who are the "elect temporary residents" and "who have been chosen and destined by *God the Father* and sanctified by the *Spirit* to be obedient to *Jesus Christ* and to be sprinkled with his blood" (1 Pet. 1:2, emphasis added). The Father who effectively calls, the Son whose very death ransoms the believers from their sinful conditions, and the Spirit who makes them holy and protects them—that community reaches into Asia Minor with a community-forming atoning work.

Self-identity

Second, Peter's focus is to create a community *self-identification* that is shaped as the people of God, a people of God that both continues and expands and extends the Israelite people of God. Here is 1 Peter 2:9-10:

> But you are a chosen race, a royal priesthood, a holy nation, God's own people, in order that you may proclaim the mighty acts of him who called you out of darkness into his marvelous light.
> Once you were not a people,
>   but now you are God's people;
> once you had not received mercy,
>   but now you have received mercy.

Each of these phrases can be unpacked, but that is not necessary here. We can simply ruminate on these categories. What Peter's communities of faith are is "Christians" (4:16), individual persons who are living out the life of Jesus in Asia Minor as part of a community of faith.

Missional Praxis

With these two observations in hand we now discuss what atonement as missional praxis means for Peter. Above all, his Trinitarian and self-identified communities are to be noted by "love." The Spirit who sanctifies creates not just individualistic Christians but a community in which love redemptively creates fellowship. Notice these words from 1 Peter 1:22-25:

> Now that you have purified your souls by your obedience to the truth so that you have genuine mutual love, love one another deeply from the heart. You have been born anew, not of perishable but of imperishable seed, through the living and enduring word of God. For
> "All flesh is like grass
>   and all its glory like the flower of grass.
> The grass withers,
>   and the flower falls,
> but the word of the Lord endures forever."
> That word is the good news that was announced to you.

What needs to be seen is the direction of this work of God: God's Spirit purifies so that they will have a "genuine mutual love" and so that they can "love one another deeply from the heart." How so? Their new birth is from the word that is a "gospel"/ "good news" and that very word is designed to create a community of love for one another. In other words, the gospel itself creates a loving community. The gospel restores cracked Eikons with God, with self, and with others—so that they can be missionally involved with one another in the world.

At this point I must not go on without (re)considering briefly the brilliant suggestion of LeRon Shults. In his coauthored book with Steven Sandage, Shults discusses forgiveness and salvation and contends that the biblical writers are less concerned with the classical *ordo salutis* than with what he calls the *salutary ordering* of persons in community.[3] That is, the gospel itself is an ecclesial, atoning work: it works to create a community in which cracked Eikons are healed in their relations with God, self, others, and the world. Herein is the telic heart of atonement: *God provides atonement in order to create a fellowship of persons who love God and love others, who find healing for the self, and who care about the world.*

For the World

And that world is the last point we need to consider about Peter's own emerging theology of survival. Readers of 1 Peter should be shocked, for I suggest that Peter's first readers were probably shocked. They were powerless and socially ostracized, and still Peter's suggestion is not to "turn and burn," as we find in some Christian literature, but to "face" the Roman Empire with the face of God in the face of Jesus Christ as the Spirit inspires that community to face itself and the world. As Bruce Winter has pointed out, the Petrine parishes were to be known—and this is what ought to shock us today—as *benefactors* within the community. Peter's words are technical: he tells his churches to "do good" (cf. 1 Pet. 2:14-15), which is the language of civic benefaction. What did Peter have in mind when he urged his communities of faith to be benefactors to the community?

> Benefactions included supplying grain in times of necessity by diverting the grain-carrying ships to the city, forcing down the price by selling it in the market below the asking rate, erecting public buildings or adorning old buildings with marble revetments such as in Corinth, refurbishing the the-

atre, widening roads, helping in the construction of public utilities, going on embassies to gain privileges for the city, and helping the city in times of civil upheaval.[4]

If I am accurate in agreeing with many today that Peter's churches were composed of the socially ostracized, we are driven to think of other aspects to benefaction—like doing whatever they could afford—but the point is the same: Peter envisions a community of faith that *creates opportunity for atonement by living a gospel life that is itself atoning*. The fellowship of the Christians created a community wherein true justice was worked out, wherein healthy, loving relationships were the norm, and wherein response to the society was one of benefaction and compassion.

But this benefactory facing of the Roman Empire is the flip side of facing one another in loving fellowship within the community, and herein lies Peter's emphasis: they are to love *one another*. "Honor everyone," Peter says, but "Love the family of believers" (1 Pet. 2:17). "Finally, all of you, have...love for one another" (3:8) and "Above all, maintain constant love for one another, for love covers a multitude of sins" (4:8). Even their greetings were special: "Greet one another with a kiss of love" (5:14).

Such a fellowship has many characteristics, not the least of which is *healed social relations*: "Rid yourselves, therefore, of all malice, and all guile, insincerity, envy, and all slander" (1 Pet. 2:1). In particular: "Finally, all of you, have unity of spirit, sympathy, love for one another, a tender heart, and a humble mind. Do not repay evil for evil or abuse for abuse; but, on the contrary, repay with a blessing. It is for this that you were called—that you might inherit a blessing" (3:8-9). Such a fellowship *flees the sinful, debauched form of "fellowship" found among the pagans*: "You have already spent enough time in doing what the Gentiles like to do, living in licentiousness, passions, drunkenness, revels, carousing, and lawless idolatry" (4:3). The fellowship is *animated by God's spiritual gifts and focuses on the good of this fellowship*:

> Above all, maintain constant love for one another, for love covers a multitude of sins. Be hospitable to one another without complaining. Like good stewards of the manifold grace of God, serve one another with whatever gift each of you has received. Whoever speaks must do so as one speaking the very words of God; whoever serves must do so with the strength that God supplies, so that God may be glorified in all things through Jesus Christ. (4:8-11)

122

Such a fellowship is not without leadership, and Peter exhorts the elders to be exemplary servants (5:1-7).

If I may be so bold to speak for Peter: his vision is (1) of a community that has been drawn into the *perichoretic* community of the Trinity, (2) that redemptively creates gracious healing of relations with one another, and (3) that, as a redemptive community of fellowship, faces the Roman Empire with the face of love and grace and peace and benefaction. The line between the Petrine parishes and the Roman Empire may exist but there are open windows and open doors and folks reaching out and drawing others into that *perichoretic* community by being a community that draws its life not from the power structures of Rome but from the *perichoretic* circle of God.

If atonement is praxis, that praxis begins in fellowship with God through the community of faith. That fellowship creates, as we will see in the next chapter, a society marked by justice.

CHAPTER
SIXTEEN

ATONEMENT AS MISSIONAL
PRAXIS: JUSTICE

We have a social gospel. We need a systematic theology large enough to match it and vital enough to back it. . . . The social gospel is the old message of salvation, but enlarged and intensified.

—Walter Rauschenbusch[1]

Before we look at atonement as the work of God that creates a pervasively just society, let me clarify the expression "social justice." We make a serious mistake when we write with adjectives: "social" before justice limits justice and moves justice from the church into the government. I propose that we drop the word "social" in the term "social justice." First, such an expression tends to imply an old-fashioned dualistic spirituality in which some things are spiritual and some things are social. In addition, the only way to define "justice" is by reference to a standard. Social justice tends to be defined by its standard: the fundamental principles of the U.S. Constitution—or a watered-down version thereof. But justice for the *Christian* is not about freedom or liberty, rights, individualism, or the pursuit of personal happiness. When that is what justice means to the Christian, that Christian has adopted Western values as the standard by which justice is defined. Christians can't let the U.S. Constitution (or John Stuart Mill or Karl Marx) define what "justice" means. We have to define justice in a way consistent with what Jesus meant by "kingdom." Which raises a postmodern issue that cuts sharply into the deep caverns of what we mean by justice.

Kant taught that universal reason would lead us to a universal sense of justice, and then more recently John Rawls suggested rather hopefully that the consensus of reasonable people would lead us to a deeper sense of justice. But postmodernists and anti-postmodernists (like Hauerwas) have entered the fray to observe that justice does not come from answering

"What is justice?" but that justice comes from those who are willing to ask "Whose justice is it?" That is, when justice is defined by some party, the power of that party's definition determines the meaning of justice. Which is to say that justice is shaped by one's moral standards, and those in power get to do the most shaping.

I accept the postmodern critique, and I add the Christian view to the mix.[2] I contend that a Christian sense of justice is one shaped by the Christian story. And that means that a Christian sense of justice is shaped by love of God and love of others instead of a Western, individualized, and modernist concept of freedom and rights. Lesslie Newbigin spoke about the supposedly self-evident truth that "every human being has an equal right to the pursuit of happiness. What this affirms," he continued, "is the right to the pursuit of happiness, not to the pursuit of the end for which humans, as a matter of fact, exist."[3] We might have rights for happiness, but what makes humans happy is not determined necessarily by having those rights. We need to ask again what a Christian theory of justice looks like.

Justice Redefined

Justice in the Bible is behavior that conforms to God's standard, and we can plumb that standard in any number of ways—through detailed analysis of specific passages in the Torah, through summaries of the Torah, through the teachings of Jesus, or through the Spirit-inspired life. Permit me two definitions: let us define justice as behavior that conforms to the teachings of Jesus and, at the same time, as behavior that emerges from the Spirit's direction. You can have it either way for, if I am right, these definitions end up at the same place. Justice is also structural at some level: it refers to the establishment of conditions that promote loving God and loving others or living in the Spirit. For the follower of Jesus, justice is not defined by the Magna Carta, the U.S. Constitution, Kant's categorical imperative, or any other social formation of law. It is defined by Jesus and by the Spirit—and we learn of its Spirit-directedness through the Bible.

Some will say that this is too religious, that it is too Christian, or that it is not practicable for a pluralistic society. I care about none of those criticisms, not because I don't think working in the public square requires common sense and even agreement on the U.S. Constitution for amicable discourse, but because we need as Christians to recover what we think the Bible says "justice" really is: the conditions that obtain when humans are right with God, with self, with others, and with the world.

We can speak, then, of "systemic justice" and we can speak of "systemic injustice." But by those we do not mean the presence or absence of freedom or of rights but instead the presence or absence of responsibility to God, to self, to others, and to the world, as the Spirit intends for each person to know. In a secular and secularizing society, in a pluralist and pluralizing culture, of course, we are not suggesting that we impose the Jesus creed or life in the Spirit on anyone, but we are asking that Christians learn to define justice by the standard that is Christian.

"Whose justice?" really is the question Christians need to wrestle with more often.

Any theory of atonement that does not have as its goal creating a society swimmingly happy in this kind of justice is not a biblical theory of atonement. If we begin (and I repeat myself) with sin as guilt, and redemption as focused on the individual, we just might pursue the Western dream of freedom, rights, and happiness. But if we begin with sin as the willing diminishment of relational love with God, self, others, and the world, and if we define atonement as the work of God to restore cracked Eikons in those four directions, then justice is also redefined: it entails a life of relational love for God, self, others, and the world. Love of God, self, others, and the world *is what is right.*

Which leads to a major front that storms through any worldly sense of justice: justice in the Bible begins with an act of God's creative, gracious forgiveness and healing. Justice in the Bible is not just deconstruction and construction, but creative, regenerating grace. Which leads to the flip side for humans: Christian behavioral justice begins in the same way—with humans creating justice through grace, forgiveness, and love. I cannot emphasize this enough, even if in what follows I cannot focus on it—I want to deal more directly with the impact of this creative grace in how justice is established in this world. But we will never see justice in the biblical sense if we fail to begin with grace and forgiveness.

The disestablishment of injustice and systemic injustices as well as the establishment of justice and systemic justices are in their own way atoning acts, for through these acts the floodgates of relationship open for humans to be restored to God, to one another, to self, and to the world.

The Bible and Justice

Our central idea needs to be put on the table before the discussion begins and it is this: the intent of God's redemptive, atoning work is to create a society wherein justice is not only established in law but also lived out by breathing, feeling human beings.

Before we get to a particularly insightful text about this in the Bible, namely Isaiah, we need to observe that the first thing God did with Abraham was to form a community of faith, lead them through the Egyptian mess and out of it, and then set up a society with a constitution at Sinai. The Torah was given to *regulate the society of God's people*. If the covenant officially created that society (Exod. 19), its laws regulated that society (Exod. 20–24). Just read Exodus or Deuteronomy and you'll see that they focus on social relations and not just personal piety, ritual purity, or rules for worship. The Torah is not predominantly a religio-moral code but a socio-moral code. The prophets railed against (mostly) Israel's leaders for not living up to the Torah and for not guiding Israel into the kind of society God intended. And as we look at the Torah's big images, if there is any one word that synthesizes the Torah it is *justice* (translating words like *tsedeq* and *mishpat*).

Isaiah

Which leads to Isaiah, who is the foundational prophet behind Jesus and hence the earliest Christian communities. Three words dominate Isaiah's vision of what society will look like when "your God reigns" (52:7): faithfulness (*ne'emana*), justice (*mishpat*), and righteousness (*tsedeq*). Thus, Isaiah's famous song of the vineyard, which is God's indictment of Israel and its leaders and the society they've created, says this of God (5:7): "he expected *justice*, but saw bloodshed; *righteousness*, but heard a cry!" (emphasis added).[4] What the Lord God says will come to pass, when things are made right and the false leaders are dumped, is this:

> See, I am laying in Zion a foundation stone,
>   a tested stone,
> a precious cornerstone, a sure foundation:
>   "One who trusts will not panic."
> And I will make *justice* the line,
>   and *righteousness* the plummet. (28:16-17, emphasis added)

And one more hopeful picture of the day God reigns:

Then *justice* will dwell in the wilderness,
 and *righteousness* abide in the fruitful field.
The effect of *righteousness* will be *peace*,
 and the result of *righteousness, quietness and trust forever.*
My people will abide in a peaceful habitation,
 in secure dwellings, and in quiet resting places.
  (32:16-18, emphasis added)

When God reigns, when the kingdom comes, then society will be put to rights. The emphasis of Isaiah, not to mention every other prophet, is not on the personal revival of millions in their relationship with God but on the establishment of a society in which *justice is done and established*— done by all because the powerful oppressors will be disestablished and the true people of God will be reestablished. There is no reason here to heap up more references, for the point is clear: the vision of Isaiah is for a society of justice and peace.

The operative words are *mishpat, tsedeqah,* and *shalom.* And their primary focus is on the social conditions created by God's redemptive act that ushers in those conditions.

Justice as Ecclesial

It is this Isaianic vision that is the source for the Lukan thread we discussed earlier, namely, the prophetic vision of Mary's *Magnificat,* Zechariah's *Benedictus,* and the crisp announcements of Jesus of what his mission was all about in his inaugural sermon (4:18-19), in the Beatitudes (6:20-26), and in his answer to John (7:22). And, as I argued there, that vision comes to expression in Acts 2 and 4, in which the earliest Christians began to live out in ecclesial shape what Jesus envisioned. Once again, the vision of Jesus is a vision of justice, of peace, and of the end of the reign of the oppressors; it is no wonder that Jesus' central term is "kingdom" and that his keynote is that "our God reigns" (that is, "kingdom *of God*").

If justice and its attending words are the central core of what God's intent is for the redemption of his created order, then the atonement, I deduce, *must be connected to justice at the systemic level.* Jesus' life, death, resurrection, and his sending of the Spirit *must* be connected to that vision of God's redemptive intent. If the intent of God is a society of peace and justice, a society marked by loving God and loving others, then the major moments of God's work must be designed to bring about peace, justice, and love. Which means that the atoning work of God is *ecclesially* shaped: it is about restoring relationships with God, with self, with others, and with the world *by creating a community in which those relationships are healed.*

I suggest again that this is exactly what Acts 2 and 4 are all about. The little flock of Jesus followers hanging out in Jerusalem, who are cemented together through fellowship and who live out justice by actively sharing goods and speaking with boldness against systemic injustices, is the remnant that will actualize the kingdom of God on earth. The great debate of Acts 15, when the leading lights of the day weighed in on who should count in the church, cannot be reduced to the conditions upon which one is acceptable to God. Instead, that debate concerned who makes up the people of God. Will it be just Jewish converts to Jesus or will it also be Gentiles who convert? Peter's decisive words in Acts 15:16-17 (quoting Amos 9:11-12) concern the rebuilding of the fallen house of David, which means including Gentiles with Jews in the people of God. His concern is *ecclesial justice for Gentiles.*

> After this I will return,
> and I will rebuild the dwelling of David, which has fallen;
> from its ruins I will rebuild it,
> and I will set it up,
> so that *all other peoples may seek the Lord—*
> *even all the Gentiles* over whom my name has been called.
> Thus says the Lord, who has been making these things
> known from long ago. (emphasis added)

This new movement, in the hands of Paul's theology, gets a new name, the *ecclesia*, but it too has the same vision: a society in which God's vision will be accomplished. Instead of oppression, there is fellowship; instead of hierarchy, there is spiritual giftedness; instead of abusive power, there are the twin powers of love and sacrifice (1 Cor. 12–14). The bringing together of the two main people groups, Jews and Gentiles, into such a society is not accidentally called "justification" (Rom. 1–3), or the making right through the formation of that very society that God intends. This theme, the inclusion of Gentiles, is also from (Second) Isaiah (55:3-5), and it is Israel who will be the agent of extending God's covenant to the nations:

> Incline your ear, and come to me;
> listen, so that you may live.

129

I will make with you an everlasting covenant,
    my steadfast, sure love for David.
See, I made him a witness to the peoples,
    a leader and commander for the peoples.
See, you shall call *nations* that you do not know,
    and *nations* that do not know you shall run to you,
because of the LORD your God, the Holy One of Israel,
    for he has glorified you. (emphasis added)

In other terms, the servant Israel (49:6), a cipher for the messianic vision, will bring this about (42:1-4):

Here is my servant, whom I uphold,
    my chosen, in whom my soul delights;
I have put my spirit upon him; ·
    he will bring forth *justice to the nations*.
He will not cry or lift up his voice,
    or make it heard in the street;
a bruised reed he will not break,
    and a dimly burning wick he will not quench;
he will faithfully bring forth justice.
He will not grow faint or be crushed
    until he has established justice in the earth;
    and the coastlands wait for his teaching. (emphasis added)

The First Evangelist, Matthew, says that this passage describes Jesus' very own missional praxis when healing folk of diseases (Matt. 12:15-21).

If justice is the heart of God's vision for his redemptive work, we are bound to see the *ecclesia* as the alternative society in which those who are "called out" of oppressive societies live that vision out. Inherent to this vision, lived out by Jesus in his table fellowship praxis, is the inclusion of Gentiles to form a new people of God.

And we are similarly bound to think that this society will spread justice in this world. Nothing could be clearer from the prophetic denunciations of Jesus against the leaders (Matt. 23), Peter's revolutionary, insubordinate response to the Jerusalem officials (Acts 4–5) and his summons of the Asia Minor parishes to live the gospel responsibly, and Stephen's prophetic explanation of what God was doing through Jesus (Acts 7:51–8:3)—and what else could be said about the apostle Paul's relentless preaching of the gospel to the Gentiles? Jesus and his many followers created an alternative society, but not simply in a sectarian sense. Instead, they took their message of the kingdom of God, the ecclesial body, into the public square as both proclamation and performance.

The Roots of Christian Justice

The roots of the Christian fight for justice are deeply embedded in Torah and the prophets, and we can but observe a few texts. I begin with Jeremiah's stinging questions directed at Shallum (a.k.a. Jehoahaz), son of Josiah, to get him to see that love of God and love of the oppressed are intertwined:

> Woe to him who builds his house by unrighteousness,
>   and his upper rooms by injustice;
> who makes his neighbors work for nothing,
>   and does not give them their wages;
> who says, "I will build myself a spacious house
>   with large upper rooms,"
> and who cuts out windows for it,
>   paneling it with cedar,
>   and painting it with vermilion.
> Are you a king
>   because you compete in cedar?
> *Did not your father eat and drink*
>   *and do justice and righteousness?*
>   *Then it was well with him.*
> He judged the cause of the poor and needy;
>   then it was well.
> *Is not this to know me?*
>   says the LORD.
> But your eyes and heart
>   are only on your dishonest gain,
> for shedding innocent blood,
> and for practicing oppression and violence. (Jer. 22:13-17,
>   emphasis added)

Jesus' own description of the judgment moves in the same direction of concern for the world—for the poor and the oppressed (Matt. 25:37-40):

> Then the righteous will answer him, "Lord, when was it that we saw you hungry and gave you food, or thirsty and gave you something to drink? And when was it that we saw you a stranger and welcomed you, or naked and gave

you clothing? And when was it that we saw you sick or in prison and visited you?" And the king will answer them, "Truly I tell you, just as you did it to one of the least of these who are members of my family, you did it to me."

Someone has said that worldliness is living in a committed way to wrong principles. The people of God—Israel, the church—is in contrast to the world: it is the world organized on right principles. And those right principles involve, as Jesus makes so clear in the Lukan kingdom thread, justice and peace and love of others. A thoroughly biblical understanding of atonement, then, is earthy. It is about restored relations with God and with self, but also with others and with the world—in the here and now.

And the apostle Paul, from whom the individualistic gospel has been wrung, is at odds at times with those who read him this way. Notice these words, which are too easily shifted into personal battles with the demons and devils, but which have become the watchwords for those fighting systemic injustice (Eph. 6:10-17):

> Finally, be strong in the Lord and in the strength of his power. Put on the whole armor of God, so that you may be able to stand against the wiles of the devil. For our struggle is not against enemies of blood and flesh, but against the rulers, against the authorities, against the cosmic powers of this present darkness, against the spiritual forces of evil in the heavenly places. Therefore take up the whole armor of God, so that you may be able to withstand on that evil day, and having done everything, to stand firm. Stand therefore, and fasten the belt of truth around your waist, and put on the breastplate of righteousness. As shoes for your feet put on whatever will make you ready to proclaim the gospel of peace. With all of these, take the shield of faith, with which you will be able to quench all the flaming arrows of the evil one. Take the helmet of salvation, and the sword of the Spirit, which is the word of God.

What Paul opposes here is the cracked systems created by powerful cracked Eikons when they together oppress powerless cracked Eikons. The Revelation of St. John, regardless of the sort of eschatology one brings to the text, is driven by two themes: that someday God will establish justice and that this justice will be established, ironically, by the Lamb, the one who suffered injustice, who will be on the throne, reversing every form of unjust power ever seen.

Conclusion

It is time now to draw these threads together. Since sin is the multifaceted distortion of humans in their relations with God, self, others, and the world, and since cracked Eikons create systemic injustice, inherent to the atoning work of God is restorative justice. God's redemptive intent is to restore and rehabilitate humans in their relationship with God, self, others, and the world, and when that happens *justice is present and established.* The followers of Jesus both proclaim and embody atoning justice by fighting injustice and establishing just that kind of justice. Their forward guard is surrounded with the banner of grace and forgiveness.

One thing becomes clear: the sense of justice in the Bible is *altogether and unabashedly relational.* I tie together now this discussion with three terms drawn from three scholars: F. LeRon Shults, Miroslav Volf, and Chris Marshall. Shults sees salvation and atonement as occurring through the image of the *face*: God's face in the Father, Son, and Spirit who smiles upon the world and invites its people to healing by pondering and receiving that face so that they can face themselves, others, and the world. Miroslav Volf works with the idea of others and the problem of exclusion that can only be resolved through *embrace.* He says, "within social contexts, truth and justice are unavailable outside of the *will to embrace* the other."[5] And Chris Marshall relentlessly exposes the meaning of justice in the Bible to demonstrate that it is relational and that God's justice-making is *restoration.* Justice, then, cannot be reduced (though it often is) to revenge or retribution. Instead, it is the redemptive grace of God at work in God's community of faith that preemptively strikes with grace, love, peace, and forgiveness to restore others to selves, and to restore selves to others.[6]

I end with Volf: "But if we see human beings as children of the one God, created by God to belong all together as a community of love, then there will be good reasons to let embrace—love—define what justice is."[7]

CHAPTER
SEVENTEEN

ATONEMENT AS MISSIONAL PRAXIS: MISSIONAL

[Emerging churches] do not believe in evangelistic strategies, other than the pursuit to be like Jesus in his interactions with others. They do not target people or have an agenda but rather seek to love all those whom God brings to them. They do not hope for a belief change for their conversation partners as much as a life change. Because of their high level of engagement with other cultures, the sacred/secular split is overcome as they practice the kingdom in their midst, in community.

—Eddie Gibbs and Ryan Bolger[1]

Missional," a word much in vogue in emerging circles as a "generous third way"[2] beyond evangelism and social action, is not simply the politically correct alternative to "evangelism." God and the gospel have *direction*. As God's direction is loving embrace within the Trinity, so the direction of the gospel is the flow of God's grace toward humans and then from human to human and from humans to the world.

Evangelism, as popularly understood and sometimes publicly maligned, traditionally focuses on one element of our hyperrelational distortion (relation to God) and it also tends to focus on one of the moments of atonement (the death of Jesus Christ). A missional approach summons the church to offer healing in relations with God, self, others, and the world, and it does so by letting each of the moments of atonement speak. So when we speak of being missional we are speaking of something larger than evangelism or, better yet, we are speaking of evangelism in a new voice.

Missional work is *atoning*. Atonement is the work God calls the church to do in its praxis of healing:

in **fellowship** (where we are healed with one another);

in **justice** (where we are healed with the world); and

in **missional** presence and activism (where we engage others to be healed through the story of Jesus).

Missional and *Missio Dei*

The foundation for using the term "missional" comes from papal statements like *Lumen Gentium* and from the Gospel and Our Culture Network (www.gocn.org), as well as from missiologists like David Bosch and Lesslie Newbigin.[3] The guiding theme is the notion of *missio Dei*: God is a missionary God, the church *is* mission, and the church has no mission but the "mission of God." Another way of saying this is that there is a church *because of* the *missio Dei*, which draws the church into God's missional work of redemption. In the words of David Bosch, "*Missio Dei* enunciates the good news that God is a God-for-people."[4] God's people inevitably become a community-for-people as they participate in the *missio Dei*.

Missional presence and activity is nothing more than participation in the missio Dei *and that participation is the praxis of atonement.* We do not ask "What missionary work can we do?" but instead "What missionary work is God doing and how can I join in?" The implications of this for atonement, especially for the praxis of atonement, are enormous. Besides the need for sensitive discernment of God's activity in the world, if we also begin our task with the *missio Dei* we discover that we reorient and revitalize everything we do. As Brian McLaren, who has helped many to see the missional focus of the church, puts it: "Jesus comes with saving love for the world. He creates the church as a missional community to join him in his mission of saving the world. He invites me to be part of this community to experience his saving love and participate in it."[5]

Another important word here is *holism*, for holism is at the heart of being missional: a *missio Dei* foundation for missional presence and work is a commitment to a whole gospel for whole people for the whole world— heart, soul, mind, strength, for everyone. God has chosen to give this work to the church, and that catholic body finds expression in each "local" community of faith wherever two or three are gathered in the name of Jesus.

As a college student I read Bonhoeffer's *Letters and Papers from Prison*, not always knowing at times what he actually meant—but his vision of the church gave rise to elements of the emerging missional, or *missio Dei*, focus we now are discovering. In about August of 1944 he said this and I underlined these words in (what is now) my tattered copy:

> The church is the church only when it exists for others. To make a start, it should give away all its property to those in need. The clergy must live sole-

ly on the free-will offerings of their congregations, or possibly engage in some secular calling. The church must share in the secular problems of ordinary human life, not dominating, but helping and serving. It must tell men of every calling what it means to live in Christ, to exist for others. In particular, our own church will have to take the field against the vices of *hubris*, power-worship, envy, and humbug, as the roots of all evil. . . . It must not under-estimate the importance of human example (which has its origin in the humanity of Jesus and is so important in Paul's teaching); it is not abstract argument, but example, that gives its word emphasis and power.[6]

"Missional" versus Attractional Ecclesiologies

Before we attach the word missional to the word atonement, it might be good for us to offer a brief explanation of how the church has understood itself. It can be said that the *Eastern church* inculturated itself in a Greek world and politicized itself into ecclesiastical structures that summoned Christians and society to the local church building. It offered in its central building, the "church," a massive vision of reality. The *Western church* inculturated itself in a Roman world and also politicized itself into ecclesiastical structures that summoned Christians and society to the local church building. It, too, offered a massive vision of reality. The *Protestant church* more narrowly focused its summons to believers (those justified by faith), but it too offered a massive vision of reality.

The problem here is that each of these ecclesiologies is tempted to root the reason for the church in an *attractional mode* of being the church. The notion of an attractional mode, however rooted it might be in ancient Israel's worship center in Jerusalem and however important it is for the church to gather together regularly, falls apart in the earliest Christian texts. Instead of simply offering an attractional model of being church, the NT offers a broader *incarnational* or *missional* approach to being church. Instead of simply summoning folks to the church once or twice a week, the God of the New Testament sends the (previously gathered) church into the world to witness to God's saving presence with the summons to invite others into that saving presence. In the history of the church, the missional approach was swallowed up by the attractional model, and we are now hearing calls from all over the world that the missional focus needs to be restored.

Let's not overdo this, however. There is no reason to create bipolar oppositions here. The Eastern, Western, and Protestant churches each had a missional or sending impulse. Still, few would question that the actual praxis has often been to attract folks to the "church," where the most important acts of sacrament, worship, sermon, and catechism occur.

Along with developing an attractional mode, leadership too was transformed—to speak too simplistically—from the *apostolic* missional mode into a patristic and medieval *priestly* mode, which was then reshaped in the Reformation into a *pedagogical* mode, and which has in the last half century been further reshaped into a *professional* mode.[7] Once again, leadership in the apostolic mode was missional—even if each of the above themes finds a reason to exist within the missional. The apostles represent Jesus in the kingdom mission: their ministry was not domestic but itinerant. Such a perception of leadership is not contrary to domestic parish ministry, but sets the example of how one carries out a missional focus within that parish.

It is in the context of these attractional and professional models that emerging Christians are summoning the church back to a more incarnational and missional focus. It is my contention that the return to a missional model is at the same time a return to an atoning model of the church itself.

The New Testament Missional Church

The Sending God

Nothing is clearer in the Christology of the Fourth Gospel than that Jesus Christ is the *sent* Son of God. Thus, we list these texts (emphasis added):

> "I can do nothing on my own. As I hear, I judge; and my judgment is just, because I seek to do not my own will but the will of him who *sent* me." (5:30)

> "And the one who *sent* me is with me; he has not left me alone, for I always do what is pleasing to him." (8:29)

> "Whoever believes in me believes not in me but in him who *sent* me. And whoever sees me sees him who *sent* me." (12:44-45)

> "Very truly, I tell you, whoever receives one whom I *send* receives me; and whoever receives me receives him who *sent* me." (13:20)

"But the Advocate, the Holy Spirit, whom the Father will *send* in my name, will teach you everything, and remind you of all that I have said to you." (14:26)

"Peace be with you. As the Father has *sent* me, so I *send* you." (20:21)

The One who is sent, Jesus, is the One who sends the Spirit and also sends the disciples into the world. To be *missional* means to be caught up in the Son's and Spirit's work of being "sent" into this world, and that work emerges from the missional Father. The church is not a place to which people go, but a spiritual body that is on a mission to draw, as did Jesus, others into the One who sent him (6:44).

Sent for the Whole Person

Jesus' sending is to the totality of humanity in the totality of its need. A scan of Matthew 8–9 shows a Jesus who dealt with those who had leprosy, with the suffering servant of the Gentile centurion, with those who were sick, with those who were taken in by the fear of natural disasters, with those possessed by demons, with those who were paralyzed, with tax collectors and sinners, with a dead girl and a bleeding woman, and with those who were blind and speechless. The afflictions of these people are not ciphers for a sinful condition, but instead are the very manifestation of their need—and Jesus met them where they were and brought the missional presence of God's kingdom into their lives (Matt. 12:28).

Perhaps the clinching observation in this entire issue—made by the First Evangelist—is that *these very missional acts of Jesus are rooted in the Spirit-inspired and justice-establishing servant of Isaiah 42.* Notice Matthew 12:15-21:

> When Jesus became aware of this, he departed. Many crowds followed him, and he cured all of them, and he ordered them not to make him known. This was to fulfill what had been spoken through the prophet Isaiah:
> "Here is my servant, whom I have chosen,
> my beloved, with whom my soul is well pleased.
> I will put my Spirit upon him,
> and he will *proclaim justice* to the Gentiles.
> He will not wrangle or cry aloud,
> nor will anyone hear his voice in the streets.

> He will not break a bruised reed
>   or quench a smoldering wick
> *until he brings justice to victory.*
>   And in his name the Gentiles will hope." (emphasis added)

What I find important here is that Jesus' healings are acts of justice, and they are acts of justice *even for Gentiles* as Jesus becomes the missional embodiment of Immanuel.

Paul as Missional Apostle

The apostle Paul took his missional activity out of the land of Israel and into the Roman Empire, and this relocation of kingdom work explains both his rhetoric (ecclesiology, soteriology) as well as the relative absence of what we might today call missional actions. But close readings of Romans 13:3-7, 1 Thessalonians 4:11-12, 2 Thessalonians 3:6-13, and 1 Timothy 5:3-16 make it clear that Paul has a bigger vision in mind: the transformation of all creation. (And this is not to mention the cosmic scope of redemption in Rom. 8:18-21.) I begin with Romans 13:3-7:

> For rulers are not a terror to *good conduct*, but to bad. Do you wish to have no fear of the authority? Then do what is *good*, and you will *receive its approval*; for it is God's servant for your good. But if you do what is wrong, you should be afraid, for the authority does not bear the sword in vain! It is the servant of God to execute wrath on the wrongdoer. Therefore one must be subject, not only because of wrath but also because of conscience. For the same reason you also pay taxes, for the authorities are God's servants, busy with this very thing. Pay to all what is due them—taxes to whom taxes are due, revenue to whom revenue is due, *respect* to whom respect is due, *honor* to whom honor is due. (emphasis added)

I appeal again to the fine study of Bruce Winter, *Seek the Welfare of the City*, wherein it is shown that language of "doing good" and "honor" and "approval" emerges out of the early Christian practice of public benefaction that brought praise to the leaders—and Paul is absent here of a narrowed evangelistic subplot. Christians were to be good citizens.

When we look at the Thessalonian churches, we observe that behind them is the patronage system whereby rich folks could live off the benefactions of others as if they were clients. Thus:

For we hear that some of you are living in *idleness*, mere *busybodies*, not doing any work. Now such persons we command and exhort in the Lord Jesus Christ to *do their work quietly and to earn their own living*. Brothers and sisters, do not be weary in doing what is right. (2 Thess. 3:11-13, emphasis added)

Paul condemns in strong terms the temptation to be idlers in a patronage system, and summons each to work *so that* care could be given to even more and one's extras could be used for the benefit of others (1 Thess. 4:11-12; 2 Thess. 3:6-13). "The secular client," Winter concludes, "must now become a private Christian benefactor."[8]

And in an innovative and insightful analysis of 1 Timothy 5:3-16, Winter contends that Christians were being tempted to abuse the already-existing Roman benefaction system for widows. In the Greco-Roman world, dowries were given to ensure that a bride/wife/mother was cared for, and alongside this Gentile custom we find in the Jewish world a weekly distribution of funds for the needy and widows (e.g., Acts 2:45; 6:1). Now to 1 Timothy 5. Paul says that the Christians were to provide for widows in their own families, and he needs to call them out on this because some were neglecting their familial duties by relying on the charity of the churches. Paul will have none of it. Refusal to provide is a denial of the faith (1 Tim. 5:8)! And Paul establishes guidelines for which widows the churches were to care for: the widow was to be without relatives, sixty years old, married only one time, and known for her own benefactions and good works (5:5, 9-10).

We have good reason to think, then, that Paul's vision was a missional vision: to establish communities of faith that lived out the gospel in such a way that new creation was at work in every corner of society.

And Evangelism

Within this general missional orientation of the followers of Jesus there was plenty of what is traditionally called "evangelism." John summoned people to the river to confess sins in the watery ablutions of baptism; Jesus summoned people to follow him and to believe in him (read John's Gospel); and the earliest Christians, like Paul and Peter, not to mention the lesser-known Barnabas or John Mark, were missionaries in the classical sense that they evangelized in distant lands.

Inherent to "evangelism" is the meaning of "gospel" and the kinds of activity involved in evangelization. I have defined the gospel in *Embracing Grace* as the work of God to restore cracked Eikons in the context of a community of union with God and communion with others for the good of others and the world. Inherent to the meaning of "gospel" is a missional approach to life itself. And the way Christians evangelized varied from person to person and from time to time, but central to evangelization is the declaration that God's redemptive work of forgiving sins, putting the world to rights, and transforming reality has now occurred in Jesus Christ. And through the Holy Spirit individuals can be brought into the community of faith where embracing grace is found and where it is unleashed as a cycle of embracing grace in a missional direction.

Evangelism inevitably accompanies a missional orientation.

Missional and Atonement

And now back to our point: a missional life is *participation in atonement.* As others are brought into contact with the kingdom of God, relations with God, self, others, and the world are restored. Such atoning work is multifaceted, as David Bosch has so defined evangelism: as that

> dimension and activity of the church's mission which, by word and deed and in the light of particular conditions and a particular context, offers every person and community, everywhere, a valid opportunity to be directly challenged to a radical reorientation of their lives, a reorientation which involves such things as deliverance from slavery to the world and its powers; embracing Christ as Savior and Lord; becoming a living member of his community, the church; being enlisted into his service of reconciliation, peace, and justice on earth; and being committed to God's purpose of placing all things under the rule of Christ.[9]

CHAPTER
EIGHTEEN

ATONEMENT AS MISSIONAL PRAXIS: LIVING THE STORY OF THE WORD

Whoever, therefore, thinks that he understands the divine Scriptures or any part of them so that it does not build the double love of God and of our neighbor does not understand it at all. Whoever finds a lesson there useful to the building of charity, even though he has not said what the author may be shown to have intended in that place, has not been deceived, nor is he lying in any way. . . . However . . . if he is deceived in an interpretation which builds up charity . . . he is deceived in the same way as a man who leaves a road by mistake but passes through a field to the same place toward which the road itself leads.

—Augustine[1]

We use a variety of terms today for the role Scripture plays in the life of the community of faith, not the least of which are Scripture as "norming norm" or "revelation" or "authority" or "inerrant" or "infallible" or "inspired." Frankly, I have no reason to argue with any such words or even with the commitment to the centrality of Scripture in the life of the Christian community. I've dedicated my life to reading and teaching the Bible, and more important, I want it to direct my every step. I have an appetite to do what Eugene Peterson says is the essential command for Christian spirituality: eat this book![2]

The question is whether or not such terms define the role Scripture plays in the life of the church when it conceives of itself as a missional community. As John Goldingay, an Old Testament scholar, reminds us: "In scripture itself, then, models such as authority, inspiration, and revelation are little used to describe scripture, much less scripture as a whole."[3] What model fits? What role does Scripture play in our life of faith together? This chapter will suggest that Scripture plays an *atoning* role in the life of the church. Before we get to such a proposal, let me clear out some rubble.

Bibliolatry

I begin with the rubble called bibliolatry, the tendency for some Christians to ascribe too much to the Bible. One of the first things we need to see about the faith of Christians is that they had their Christian faith before they had the Bible. Telford Work, a gifted scholar, makes just this point:

> While the Bible is basic to Christianity, it is also marginal—in that God alone occupies the center of the faith, and that both belief in God and the believing community predate and will succeed Scripture's present form and roles.[4]

At the center of the Christian faith is the Trinity, and the gospel and atonement are about restoring cracked Eikons to this Trinitarian God. Beginning our understanding of Scripture with the Trinity is to claim the personal nature of everything Christian. Whenever the Bible replaces the Trinity, we have bibliolatry. The first Christians believed that God's story entered a new chapter with Jesus, and they were living in that story before they sat down to write it. So we need to get this straight: our faith finds expression in Scripture but that faith is in the Trinitarian God and not in the Bible. Our faith is in the Bible in the sense that in it we hear the Trinitarian God whom we have come to know. I do not think that we can know the Trinitarian God apart from what we learn of him through the church's Bible, but even conceding this allows us to keep God front and center in terms of what Scripture is.

Understanding the priority of the Trinity allows us to say that Scripture is the extension of the Trinity into our world. We begin with God and not with Scripture, even though we know God through Scripture. God the Father sends his very own Son, and his Son sends his Spirit to create the church, and Scripture is an expression of the Spirit's presence in the church. Here is the proper order and it reverses the method of many:

Father → Son → Spirit → Church → Scripture

Of course, we know God through Scripture, but I think that we can be even more accurate if we say this: we know God through the Spirit who makes God known through Scripture.

Lest I be accused of saying something out of bounds, let me offer an illustration. I am an avid reader of biographies, one of which is Jean Cash's sparkling biography of Flannery O'Connor.[5] If I were to treat Jean Cash's story of O'Connor the way many treat the Bible, I would focus my efforts on her text—how she told the story, how she arranged her facts, how she "story-fied" O'Connor, and how her story compares to and contrasts with other stories of O'Connor. Then I would have to investigate more about Jean Cash and her family of origin and friends and scholarly career and influences, and before long I could either reconstruct or deconstruct her story.

But there is a better way. I could read Cash to come to know O'Connor, however imperfectly, and this would lead me to read O'Connor herself so I could know her even more. Which, should you care to know, is what happened when I read Cash's studious biography.

So also with Scripture: we read Scripture not to know Scripture better and more (though some clearly do this) but to know God more and better. *The reason we do this is because Scripture is the voice of God that leads us to God.* Scripture is an agent of atonement in our relationship to God. Defeating bibliolatry, especially with the chest-thumping dogmatism that I sometimes hear among my fellow emerging Christians, is a pyrrhic victory if it is not at the same time a surrender to what the Bible is—the word of God for the church in its generation as the word from God that restores cracked Eikons (but more of that soon).

Cognitive Behaviorists

A second piece of rubble that needs to be removed gets me in trouble with my own profession and my closest friends. Briefly put, cognitive behaviorists teach that if we get things right in our mind we will behave accordingly. With respect to spiritual formation, then, the theory goes like this: the more Bible we learn, the better Christians we should be; the more theology we grasp, the better we will live. Before I say something ridiculous for some of my readers, let me make it clear that I'm a Bible-believing and theologically informed evangelical moderate (I could add a few more labels if needed). But we also need to make this clear: *knowing more Bible doesn't necessarily make me a better Christian.* I've hung around with enough nasty Bible scholars and enough mean-spirited pastors to know that knowing more Bible does not inevitably create a better Christian. And I've known plenty of loving Christians who don't know the difference between Matthew and John, let alone the differences between Kings and Chronicles.

The cognitive behaviorist approach denies a biblical theory of the

Eikon. We are made as Eikons, we cracked the Eikon (through our will), and the resolution of the problem of cracked Eikons is not simply through the mind. It is through the will, the heart, the mind, and the soul—and the body, too. No matter how much Bible we know, we will not be changed until we give ourselves over to what Augustine called "faith seeking understanding." The way of Jesus is personal, and it is relational, and it is through the door of loving God and loving others. The mind is a dimension of our love of God (heart, soul, mind, and strength), but it is not the only or even the first door to open.

Scripture is more than information revealed for our knowledge so that, in knowing more, we will be more. In fact, Scripture is God's word for God's people so that in hearing this word in communion with others we learn how to walk in this world in the way of Jesus.

Scripture, Church, and Identity-shaping

There is one more piece of rubble that needs to be cleared away. Scripture, if my order is right, is the *church's book*. Father, Son, Spirit, Church, Scripture—if this is the order, we get Scripture through the church. Now this has a very important implication for each one of us, especially for those of us who are trained to be Scripture experts, especially for those of us who delight in finding something someone has never seen before. Scripture is the *church's* story of Jesus and that means that it is designed to be read and interpreted within the community of faith as it interacts with both the church's tradition and contemporary culture.

Now we have arrived at our central concern in this section: *Scripture is the Spirit-inspired story of Jesus as communicated through, to, and for the church.* As such, the New Testament, and in its wake a fresh understanding of Hebrew Scriptures, is the church's story of Jesus Christ. By "story" I mean that the Bible comes to us in an overarching narrative that begins with creation and charts a path through the covenant with Abraham, the exodus under Moses, the kingdom under David, the attempt to live out the covenant in the land that quickly falls apart into the division of Israel, the necessary rise of the prophetic summons to live within the covenant, the seemingly inevitable exile, and the revival-like return to the land to reestablish worship and obedience to the Torah. It is this story—the Creator God forming a covenant with a community of faith (Israel) in this world, shaping his redemption in terms of exodus and worship (including atoning sacrifices), and willingly guiding a free people who at times need discipline—that is continued and fulfilled in the story of Jesus himself, who continues that very same story in the church that is his body.

But this story is the *church's story of Jesus Christ; it is the church's story of the development of Israel's story*. It is nothing other than the church's story of nothing other than Israel's story as fulfilled in no other than Jesus Christ and continued in no other than the Spirit. The church's story has one intent: *to shape the identity of God's people, and therefore every one of God's people*. The church invites everyone to learn this story and to let this story become each person's story. Some prefer to speak of the Scriptures with terms such as "authority," and as I have said above, I have no problem with such a term, but I don't think that is the best term to use for the Christian's (or non-Christian's) relationship to Scripture, just as I do not think "authority" is the best term to describe my relationship to my students or my relationship to my pastor.

The best way to describe Scripture is that it is *identity-shaping*. The Bible tells us who we are, where we are, and where we are going. In fact, its identity-shaping, Spirit-mentored direction propels its readers into a missional life. Eugene Peterson warns of the danger of making the Bible after our own Trinitarian image: my Holy Wants, Holy Needs, and Holy Feelings. Instead, if we read the Bible aright, we are remade—since the Bible has been sent as a word from God to us—into God's image, the perfect Eikon, Jesus Christ.[6]

Scripture as Missional

Scripture is inherently *missional* and praxis oriented. This is nowhere clearer than in the early Christian statement in 2 Timothy 3:15-17:[7]

> and how from childhood you have known the sacred writings that are able to instruct you for salvation through faith in Christ Jesus. All [or, better yet, *Every (text of)*] scripture is inspired by God and is useful for teaching, for reproof, for correction, and for training in righteousness, *so that everyone who belongs to God may be proficient, equipped for every good work*. (emphasis added)

Great debates rage over the meaning of "inspired" (Greek *theopneustos*), but, since the term is so rare, it is best to keep it general and obvious: every text in Scripture is a "God-spirited" text and therefore different from any other text. As God-spirited stuff, Scripture (all of it) is "useful" (*ophelimos*) for those who let it have its Spirit-directed way—and useful in these four (missional) directions: teaching, reproof, correction, and training in righteousness. And it is useful for these four things "so that" Christians, those who belong to God (who "spirits" the Bible), might be "equipped for every good work."

This is what it is meant by Scripture being *missional*: Scripture is designed by God to work its story into persons of God so that they may become doers of the good. Scripture is missional because it is designed to create restored Eikons who are in union with God and communion with others *for the good of others and the world*. Scripture, I sometimes have to tell myself, is not designed just to be exegeted and probed and pulled apart until it yields its (gnostic-like) secrets to those who know its languages and its interpretive traditions and who can then divulge their gleanings behind pulpits on Sunday mornings or in monographs and academic journals (very few care to read).

Scripture is missional because it is designed to create missional people who learn from their missional praxis how to see Scripture as a missional text that shapes them so that they can live in the story that the church tells in Scripture. To use the terms of Kevin Vanhoozer in his massive *The Drama of Scripture*, Scripture is a "theo-dramatic script" that is performed by the people of God on the world's historical stage.

To say that the church's Scripture is missional, to say that it is a theo-dramatic script, is to bring us back one more time to atonement as praxis: when Scripture is treated as missional, Scripture restores cracked Eikons in all four directions—with God, with the self, with others, and with the world. Scripture as story heals a wounded people and wounded persons. Even if in a slightly different order, Telford Work's study *Living and Active* contends much the same when he frames Scripture as follows:

> Our bibliology [his word for the theology of Scripture] starts where the Bible starts: in the eternal purposes of the Triune God. It goes where the Bible goes: out to the fallen world as God's instrument and medium. [Here, the missional intent.] And it ends where the Bible ends: in the eternal assembly of the Triune God's worshiping disciples.[8]

Central to my understanding of atonement is the notion of *identification for incorporation*: Jesus identifies with us—in the incarnation—so that we can identify with Jesus. He lives our life so that we can live his life. The apostle Paul calls this both co-crucifixion and co-resurrection, and it reveals that Jesus' story is to become our story as we identify with him and we are incorporated into him. Notice Galatians 2:19-20:

147

I have been crucified with Christ; and it is no longer I who live, but it is Christ who lives in me. And the life I now live in the flesh I live by faith in the Son of God, who loved me and gave himself for me.

Or Romans 6:11: "So you also must consider yourselves dead to sin and alive to God in Christ Jesus." If we add to this that the co-crucified and co-resurrected are also mutually indwelled by the Spirit of God, we have in front of us a perfect model of learning how to enter the story of Jesus in Scripture. We are invited to identify with Jesus, to let his story be our story, *by dying to self, by being raised to new life with Christ, and by being overcome by the grace of God's Spirit* to become, through this missionally shaped and atoning story, people who are equipped for every good work.

The church becomes a community called atonement every time it reads the story of Jesus and every time it identifies itself with that story and every time it invites others to listen in to hear that story. Reading Scripture and listening to Scripture and letting Scripture incorporate us into its story is atoning.

CHAPTER NINETEEN

ATONEMENT AS MISSIONAL PRAXIS: BAPTISM, EUCHARIST, AND PRAYER

[Sacrifice] has the effect of linking the sacramental rituals of both baptism and Eucharist to the story of Jesus, and thus to the theology of the atonement: baptism is a once-for-all immersion into Christ's death and resurrection; Eucharist is a repeated participation in the benefits of Christ's passion.
—Stephen Sykes[1]

We are contending in this last section of the book that the community of faith is a community of atonement. This is seen in its missional focus, its fellowship within and without, its striving for justice in all directions, its extension of the gospel of atonement to others, and its praxis of reading and identifying with the story of Scripture. But there are three other specific practices that shape how the church lives out atonement: baptism, Eucharist, and prayer. We need to look at each.

Baptism and Eucharist: The Sacraments of Atonement

It is impossible here to enter into the historical discussions and debates, but I want to say this: baptism offers *purification and incorporation* and Eucharist offers an *incorporated fellowship together with God.*

Baptism

Baptism's practiced history shapes how we understand it today. The debates on whether the earliest Christians baptized infants raged between scholars decades ago. Others narrowed their focus to texts like Colossians 2:11-12, in which circumcision and baptism are tied together—making a link with infant baptism more likely. There is no reason to enter those debates here. Instead, we are interested in this question: What does baptism do?

Purification

To answer this, I think we should begin with Josephus, who had nothing whatsoever to do with the Christian faith. But if you read this text you know that he knows what baptism was about in the first century:

> But to some of the Jews the destruction of Herod's army seemed to be divine vengeance, and certainly a just vengeance, for his treatment of John, surnamed the Baptist. For Herod had put him to death, though he was a good man and had exhorted the Jews to lead righteous lives, to practise justice towards their fellows and piety towards God, and so doing to join in baptism. In his view this was a necessary preliminary if baptism was to be acceptable to God. They must not employ it to gain pardon for whatever sins they committed, but as a consecration of the body implying that the soul was already thoroughly cleansed by right behaviour.[2]

What no one contests is that John's baptism, found also in the early chapters of each of the Gospels, is the fount of Jesus' and the early Christian praxis of baptism. Josephus opens a window onto just what that was: an act of *purification*. Baptism involved conversion and confession, forgiveness and remission. What it also meant was that the temple was no longer the location to find purity; purity was found in a confessing, watery baptism that cleansed (at some level) the baptisand from his or her sins.

Such a view makes sense of a few other texts in the New Testament. John's baptism was in "living water" (running water, the Jordan River). We know from the Jewish custom of building *mikva'ot* (sacred baths) that one side was lower than the others so that, if full (which it often wasn't), water could run and be "living" and purifying. And John exhorted folks to get into the river Jordan and wash themselves clean of their sins by confessing their sins and turning to the message he had from God. Jesus joined in. He, too, believed that this watery, purifying rite would wash Israel of its sins and set it in a kingdom direction. When Jesus exhorts the man born blind to wash in the pool of Siloam (John 9:7), we see a Jewish view of things: this baptism-like washing in the pool purifies the man.

Baptism, in its earliest phase, wiped away moral dirt. This is why the early Christians connect baptism so often to moral transformation. Notice these texts:

> As many of you as were baptized into Christ have clothed yourselves with Christ. (Gal. 3:27)

> And this [list of sinful types of people] is what some of you used to be. But you were *washed*, you were sanctified, you were justified in the name of the Lord Jesus Christ and in the Spirit of our God. (1 Cor. 6:11, emphasis added)

> And baptism, which this prefigured, now saves you—not as a removal of dirt from the body, but as an appeal to God for a good conscience, through the resurrection of Jesus Christ, who has gone into heaven and is at the right hand of God, with angels, authorities, and powers made subject to him. (1 Pet. 3:21-22)

Baptism is the church's rite offered to cracked Eikons that purges and purifies Eikons from their pollutions.

Incorporation

Baptism evokes many other ideas, but what we need to observe briefly is that it not only purifies but also carries with it the sense of being *incorporated into Christ and his body*. Here is the classic text from Romans 6:1-4:

> What then are we to say? Should we continue in sin in order that grace may abound? By no means! How can we who died to sin go on living in it? Do you not know that all of us who have been baptized into Christ Jesus were baptized into his death? Therefore we have been buried with him by baptism into death, so that, just as Christ was raised from the dead by the glory of the Father, so we too might walk in newness of life.

Baptism is about being incorporated into Christ and his body. It is ecclesial and the quintessential "act of church membership." One more text from Paul, this time from 1 Corinthians 12:13: "For in the one Spirit we were all baptized into one body—Jews or Greeks, slaves or free—and we were all made to drink of one Spirit." John the Baptist also saw baptism this way: those who participated in his baptism became part of the end-time remnant, entering into the Jordan in order to cross it again as the newly covenanted twelve-tribe followers of Jesus.

Baptism is the church's rite of offering to others entrance into the waters in order to be purified so that the person can enter into union with Christ and the body of Christ. This is what *atonement* is all about. Baptism is the church's praxis-rite of atonement; it is one way that the church offers atonement to others; and it is how the church offers purification and incorporation—or restored relationship—with God, self, and others as a missional people.

Eucharist

The Eucharist is the church's sign of *incorporated fellowship with God and God's people*. We use many terms, and it doesn't matter too much which one we use in this context: Lord's Supper, Eucharist, communion, mass, or memorial feast.

Context

The Lord's Supper is the *Last* Supper because Jesus constantly practiced table fellowship with his followers, and it was during the last of these dinners that Jesus revealed a new meaning to an ordinary meal. Every evening for some three years they had gathered together, prayed, talked, ate, and talked some more. Jesus made a name for himself because of his table practices (Matt. 11:16-19). The Eucharist cannot be understood aright until it is seen as a fellowship meal.

Passover

Jesus transformed an ordinary Passover-like meal (there is, as I said earlier, considerable debate about whether the last supper was the Passover meal or not, since no lamb is mentioned) into a memorial feast of his saving death, resurrection, and promised renewal of table fellowship (Mark 14:12-31, with parallels). Here are the words that interpret this meal: "this is my body" and "my blood of the covenant" and "poured out for many" and "for the forgiveness of sins" and "new covenant." Jesus creates this meal to enable his followers to remember him for generations, not just in the sense of recall, but in the sense of reliving that night in such a manner that they participate each time in the saving effects of Jesus' death and resurrection. They both act out this meal and reappropriate its saving power each time they do this.

Ecclesial

Preeminently, the Eucharist is a community or ecclesial event. As the German scholar Gerd Theissen made clear in his seminal study *The Social Setting of Pauline Christianity*, it was a problem that the Corinthians' meals began to reflect pagan power structures rather than the radical equality of the Christian community.[3] Evidently the wealthy were simply gathering together, excluding the poor, and not carefully distinguishing ordinary meals from the Lord's Supper. So in 1 Corinthians 10–11 Paul exhorts them to eat ordinary meals at home and learn to share the Lord's Supper together. However one attempts to get behind Paul's instructions, it is clear that the Lord's Supper was an *ecclesial* meal—one that brought into visible reality the unity of the church and its constant need to feast upon the Lord's atoning work.

Praxis of Atonement

Finally, the Lord's Supper is a praxis of atonement. It reminds each person of their need to be in fellowship with Christ's atoning work, it reminds the local community of faith of its corporate need to feast upon the Lord, and it visibly declares to all that the Christian community is a community that draws its life from Jesus Christ, the crucified and resurrected Lord. By offering the Lord's Supper, the local community offers atonement. As such, we find restoration with God, with self, with others, and with the world around us. And it is not just an offering by the church to others; those who participate in the Lord's Supper participate in the atoning work of God in this world.

How Inclusive?

Which raises the question of who is permitted at the table of the Lord. The church is divided into three camps, who say either that the Eucharist is for local members or for all believers or for any who seek its blessings.

The first group restricts the table to those who are Christians, or who are "right with the Lord" (however that might be measured), or who are in that particular fellowship (closed communion), or who are members of a given denomination. Those in this group argue their case either by appeal to the expression in 1 Corinthians 11:28 ("Examine yourselves...") or to the sacredness of the meal or to Old Testament precedents or even to the commonsensical notion that early Christians were persecuted, so they would not have offered the meal to anyone but themselves. The second group sees the Lord's Supper as exclusively a Christian praxis, and therefore they restrict it to anyone who claims to be a Christian. The third group contends that, since this meal is an offer of grace, there is no better place for others to find the grace of God than at this table. If the first and second groups end up on the sticky wicket of monitoring who gets to partake, the third group throws the doors wide open to individual conscience.

Matters like these are not decided by individuals, but by local churches and leaders. I would argue from the table fellowship of Jesus, which is where I think we need to begin any discussion of the Eucharist, that the table is open to all who want to focus their attention on Jesus' death and resurrection. My own view, within proper limits, is that this is not a meal so much in need of protection as it is a meal in need of missional extension. Come, we say, and see. Come and taste. Come find grace. If a person seeks for grace, this is where we want them to come.

Why do we fling wide the doors? Because the Eucharist is a meal that offers atonement—with God, self, others, and the world.

Prayer: The Face of Atonement

Synagogues outside the land of Israel were called *proseuche*, or "houses of prayer." When churches gradually began to be built in the Roman Empire, they too were houses of prayer. The church has been, is, and always will be a place of prayer.

Prayer is *facing* God with heart, soul, mind, and strength. Prayer is also learning to face God *together*. By offering the practice of prayer to the world, the church offers folks the opportunity to face God and to face God with others, and in so facing God to become restored to God, to self, and to others. As such, prayer is atoning.

Prayer in the Christian tradition, as it unfolds out of the Jewish and early Christian praxis of prayer, is of two sorts. There is the spontaneous prayer of the individual who simply faces God wherever she is, whenever she wants, and about whatever she wants to face God about. And there is corporate prayer when a group of two or more face God together at mutually agreed-upon places and times. The first is a praxis of atonement that restores us to God in such a way that we commune with God and are healed. Prayer also creates in us the capacity to be atoning agents for others and the world. The second is a praxis of atonement that restores us to God and to self, but does so in such a way that it melds us into a community of faith. I have written about this in my book *Praying with the Church*, and so will limit myself here to the basics.[4]

The Jewish prayer tradition, like all other prayer traditions, springs from the inevitable and relentless human need to face God. The first "prayer" of Adam to God contained these words: "I heard the sound of you in the garden, and I was afraid, because I was naked; and I hid myself" (Gen. 3:10). This is the "naked" truth about a man who had suddenly learned the naked reality of sin. Genuine prayer faces God with a genuine heart; genuine prayer simply tells God what is in the heart and on the mind. The Psalms are simply that: prayers of authentic hearts and minds written down for posterity to see what genuine prayer is like. Prayers like "How long?" and "Why?" as well as "Hallelujah!" and "I will sing to the LORD, for he has triumphed gloriously; horse and rider he has thrown into the sea" (Exod. 15:1).

Alongside this spontaneous, personal, private prayer is another form of prayer in the church. It, too, emerges from the oldest of Jewish prayer practices. God tells the Israelites that each day is to begin and end with the *Shema*, from Deuteronomy 6:4-5: "Hear, O Israel: The LORD is our God, the LORD alone. You shall love the LORD your God with all your heart, and with all your soul, and with all your might." The custom of reciting the *Shema* at least twice a day gradually evolved into what appears to have been a three-times-a-day sacred rhythm of prayer for observant Jews. At daybreak, the covenant people recited the *Shema*, the Ten Commandments, and a long prayer now called the *Amidah* (eighteen separate benedictions); at the time of the afternoon sacrifice it seems that Jews paused, faced the temple, and said at least the *Amidah*, and then before retiring they said once again the *Shema*, the Ten Commandments, and the *Amidah*. Whether this is exactly what Jews did is not the point; something on this order was done to remind themselves of God's central requirements and of turning the face and heart toward God.

The early Christians developed this three-times-a-day practice into saying the Jesus creed (Mark 12:28-32), the Lord's Prayer, and perhaps even the Ten Commandments. However this developed, by the fourth

155

century Christians had developed a clear prayer custom of pausing to pray together anywhere from two to seven times a day. It would be St. Benedict, in his famous *Rule*, who would create the sacred prayer rhythm that many Christians have followed since his time.

Local communities of faith need to offer these prayer practices to the wider community. Local churches need to be places where folks can face God, with one another, in prayer. This is a praxis of atonement. In fact, the routine gathering together to "say our prayers" ties together several features of the praxis of atonement: it is fellowship with God and with others, it heals the self to be in the presence of God and God's people, it is hearing the story of the word of God, it establishes a just society wherein no distinctions are made, it can be connected to the Eucharist, and it can remind those so praying time and time again of the missional nature of God's people in this world.

It is one praxis that embodies the simple message that we are a community called atonement.

BIBLIOGRAPHIC NOTE

I have read far more books and articles than would be appropriate to cite in this context. I apologize here to authors from whom I learned but neither interact with nor cite. I also apologize to those who think I should not only have read their work (and haven't) but interacted with it as well. I'm aware of much of what I haven't read, but this is not a book about atonement theories. Instead, it proposes a way of putting atonement into a conceptual clarity. Of all I have read, I consider the following to be the most representative and significant. I omit subtitles here and in the notes.

H. Boersma, *Violence, Hospitality, and the Cross* (Grand Rapids: Baker Academic, 2004).

G. Florovsky, *Creation and Redemption* (Belmont, Mass.: Nordland, 1976).

J. Goldingay, ed., *Atonement Today* (London: SPCK, 1995).

J. B. Green, M. Baker, *Recovering the Scandal of the Cross* (Downers Grove, Ill.: IVP, 2000).

C. Gunton, *The Actuality of Atonement* (Grand Rapids: Eerdmans, 1989).

M. Heim, *Saved from Sacrifice* (Grand Rapids: Eerdmans, 2006).

R. Reno, *Redemptive Change* (Harrisburg, Penn.: Trinity, 2002).

P. Schmiechen, *Saving Power* (Grand Rapids: Eerdmans, 2005).

J. R. W. Stott, *The Cross of Christ* (Downers Grove, Ill.: IVP, 1986).

M. Volf, *Exclusion and Embrace* (Nashville: Abingdon, 1996).

J. Denny Weaver, *The Nonviolent Atonement* (Grand Rapids: Eerdmans, 2001).

NOTES

Front Matter

1. *Fracture* (Grand Rapids: Eerdmans, 2006), 271.
2. *The Politics of Jesus* (2nd ed.; Grand Rapids: Eerdmans, 1994), 52.

1. Atonement: The Question, a Story, and Our Choice

1. *Ancient-Future Faith* (Grand Rapids: Baker Books, 1999), 39, 40.
2. *Transforming Mission* (Maryknoll, N.Y.: Orbis, 1991), 399.
3. The irony of this story is that when I first wrote this up and asked for Dawn's permission, I was not aware that her daughter would become a student of mine at North Park.
4. I use "atonement" in its large sense, and this usage is common among theologians—take, for instance, the conservative evangelical theologian W. A. Grudem, *Systematic Theology* (Grand Rapids: Zondervan, 1994), 568.
5. *Divided by Faith* (Oxford: Oxford University Press, 2000), 142.

2. With Jesus, Of Course!

1. *The Secret Message of Jesus* (Nashville: W, 2006), 3.
2. I have worked this out in an academic shape in my *A New Vision for Israel* (Grand Rapids: Eerdmans, 1999), and in a more popular format in both *The Jesus Creed* (Brewster, Mass.: Paraclete, 2004) and *Embracing Grace* (Brewster, Mass.: Paraclete, 2005).
3. On this, see my book on Mary: *The Real Mary* (Brewster, Mass.: Paraclete, 2006), 102-5.
4. On whether Jesus and the earliest Christians were "postcolonial"-type thinkers, see now the fine study of Christopher Bryan, *Render to Caesar* (New York: Oxford, 2005).
5. Jesus is not against "power" per se; he is against the improper use of power. All power, he teaches, is God's and is what the Father has entrusted to him.
6. This has been explored by many today in differing ways. I mention three: J. H. Yoder, *The Politics of Jesus* (Grand Rapids: Eerdmans, 1994); S. Hauerwas, *The Peaceable Kingdom* (Notre Dame: University of Notre Dame, 1983); and D. Harink, *Paul among the Postliberals* (Grand Rapids: Brazos, 2003).

3. With God, with Eikons, and with Sin, Too

1. *Death on a Friday Afternoon* (New York: Basic, 2000), 8-9.
2. *Mere Christianity* (New York: Macmillan, 1956), 42.
3. See M. Volf, *After Our Likeness* (Grand Rapids: Eerdmans, 1998), 209 (italics his).
4. F. LeRon Shults, *Reforming Theological Anthropology* (Grand Rapids: Eerdmans, 2003), 92.
5. Theologians distinguish between the ontological Trinity, in which they focus on God's *ousia* (or being), and the economic Trinity, in which *perichoresis* can dominate the discussion. There is a danger in some theologians, who need not be mentioned here, to overdo one or the other. The focus here on *perichoresis* is because our subject matter, atonement, is shaped by this element of Trinitarian faith.
6. See his *Invitation to Theology* (Downers Grove, Ill.: IVP, 2001), 19.
7. New York: Viking, 2002.
8. *The Mind of the Maker* (San Francisco: HarperSanFrancisco, 1987), 12.
9. I rely here on J. Richard Middleton's excellent *The Liberating Image* (Grand Rapids: Brazos, 2005).
10. In *What Does It Mean to Be Saved?* (ed. J. G. Stackhouse, Jr.; Grand Rapids: Baker, 2002), 122.
11. Wayne Grudem, *Systematic Theology*, 490 (italicized in original), which is expanded upon in pp. 490-514. Grudem here stands on the shoulders of L. Berkhof, *Systematic Theology* (Grand Rapids: Eerdmans, 1941), 233: "... sin may be defined as *lack of conformity to the moral law of God, either in act, disposition, or state.*"
12. J. Rodman Williams, *Renewal Theology: God, the World & Redemption* (Grand Rapids: Zondervan, 1988), 222.
13. *Not the Way It's Supposed to Be* (Grand Rapids: Eerdmans, 1995), 13, 14, 16.
14. From the song "Me From Me" on the album *Dave Miller* © 2004 dave millermusic/ASCAP. Available at www.davemilleronline.com.
15. W. Pannenberg, *Systematic Theology* (trans. G. W. Bromiley; Grand Rapids: Eerdmans, 1994), 2.252.
16. E. Brunner, *The Christian Doctrine of Creation and Redemption* (trans. O. Wyon; Philadelphia: Westminster, 1952), 89.
17. See his *Creation and Redemption*, 92-93.

4. With Eternity, with Ecclesial Community, and with Praxis, Too

1. *Past Event and Present Salvation* (Louisville: Westminster John Knox Press, 1989), 13.

2. See now M. Volf, *The End of Memory* (Grand Rapids: Eerdmans, 2006).

3. There is a lot written about what both the Bible says and about how Christians have understood heaven. I recommend just one piece here: Jerry L. Walls, *Heaven* (New York: Oxford, 2002).

4. K. Vanhoozer, *The Drama of Doctrine* (Louisville, Ky.: WJKP, 2005); see also Hans Urs von Balthasar, *Theo-drama* (4 vols.; San Francisco: Ignatius, 1988–1994).

5. Grammatically, in 5:18 the God who reconciled us is the same God who gave us the ministry. There is one article, tying the two acts together: "the God who reconciled-and-gave." The "God was in Christ" of 5:19 is functional, but assumes the ontological.

5. Atonement as Metaphor: Metaphor and Mechanics

1. *The Actuality of Atonement* (Grand Rapids: Eerdmans, 1989), 34.

2. "The Hedgehog and the Fox: An Essay on Tolstoy's View of History," in his *The Proper Study of Mankind* (ed. H. Hardy and R. Hausheer; New York: FSG, 2000), 436-98, quoting from pp. 436, 438.

3. A brief notation on each "theory" of the atonement. Abelard contended that the cross was a demonstration of God's love to evoke a change of heart on the part of those who perceive its costly love. In Anselm's view, sin dishonors God; humans can never return the glory lost to God by their sin; someone must stand in between who is both God and human; and Jesus Christ "satisfies" that condition. Atonement is satisfaction. Incarnationists emphasize God becoming human, God identifying with humans, and God taking on mortality in order to provide life for those destined to death. Penal substitution frames atonement in terms of God's wrath against sin as the holy reaction of an all-holy God; Jesus absorbs that wrath on the cross as propitiation; and God's wrath is pacified in that act of "self-punishment." *Christus Victor* expresses the entrance of Christ into captive territory and his death and resurrection as providing the means of liberating humans from their slavery to sin, self, and Satan. Recapitulation trades on the idea that Jesus Christ recapitulated Adam's life, and therefore the life of every human, and undoes the sin and death Adam handed on to humans. Jesus' identification with humans enables humans to have a perfect redemption. For a good survey, see now Peter Schmiechen, *Saving Power* (Grand Rapids: Eerdmans, 2005); see also the debate among evangelicals in J. Beilby, P. R. Eddy, eds., *The Nature of the Atonement* (Downers Grove, Ill.: IVP, 2006).

4. A. C. Thiselton, *New Horizons in Hermeneutics* (Grand Rapids: Zondervan, 1997); K. Vanhoozer, *The Drama of Doctrine*; C. Gunton, *The Actuality of Atonement*.

5. *Actuality of Atonement*, 46, 39.

6. *The Language and Imagery of the Bible* (Philadelphia: Westminster, 1980), 152.

7. *Metaphorical Theology* (Philadelphia: Fortress, 1982), 15.

8. *Drama of Doctrine*, 30.

9. Grand Rapids: Zondervan, 1992, 351.

10. *New Horizons in Hermeneutics*, 352.

11. Frances Young, *Virtuoso Theology* (Cleveland, Ohio: Pilgrim, 1993).

12. *Violence, Hospitality, and the Cross* (Grand Rapids: Baker Academic, 2004).

13. *Violence, Hospitality, and the Cross*, 104.

14. In *The Glory of the Atonement* (ed. C. E. Hill and F. A. James III; Downers Grove, Ill.: IVP, 2004), 138.

15. In *The Nature of the Atonement* (ed. J. Beilby and P. R. Eddy; Downers Grove, Ill.: IVP, 2006), 67. Schreiner is rightfully criticized for using terms like "foundation" and "heart" and "soul" without providing anything more than explanatory rhetoric. To say that penal substitution is central requires that biblical texts are examined in which without this theory the atonement falls apart. See the responses in that volume by Greg Boyd (99-105) and Joel Green (110-16).

16. J. B. Green, M. Baker, *Recovering the Scandal of the Cross* (Downers Grove, Ill.: IVP, 2000); see now M. D. Baker, ed., *Proclaiming the Scandal of the Cross* (Grand Rapids: Baker, 2006).

17. On this, see especially T. Gorringe, *God's Just Vengeance* (Cambridge: Cambridge University Press, 1996).

18. Many have stated this. One good example is Rita Nakashima Brock, Rebecca Ann Parker, *Proverbs of Ashes* (Boston: Beacon, 2001).

19. Boulder, Colo.: Westview, 2001. I quote here from p. 12.

20. L. L. Morris, *The Apostolic Preaching of the Cross* (Grand Rapids: Eerdmans, 1972); J. R. W. Stott, *The Cross of Christ* (Downers Grove, Ill.: IVP, 1986); J. I. Packer, "What Did the Cross Achieve? The Logic of Penal Substitution," in *The J. I. Packer Collection* (ed. A. McGrath; Downers Grove, Ill.: IVP, 1999), 94-136. The piece by Packer is required reading for anyone who wants to understand penal substitution.

21. *Free of Charge* (Grand Rapids: Zondervan, 2006), 139.

22. *Free of Charge*, 140.

23. I do not know if Howard Marshall's piece is published.

6. The Mystery of Our Metaphors: An Exercise in Postmodern Humility

1. Kevin Vanhoozer, "The Atonement in Postmodernity: Guilt, Goats and Gifts," in *The Glory of the Atonement* (ed. C. E. Hill and F. A. James III; Downers Grove, Ill.: IVP, 2004), 396.

2. Subtitled *New Testament Ethics in an African American Context* (Nashville: Abingdon, 2001), 15.

3. *Rethinking Human Nature* (Grand Rapids: Baker, 2006).
4. Ted Peters, *Sin* (Grand Rapids: Eerdmans, 1994), 9.
5. Mark Biddle, *Missing the Mark* (Nashville: Abingdon, 2005); Ted Peters, *Sin*, 155.
6. *Not the Way It's Supposed to Be*, 54.
7. *The Confessions* (trans. Philip Burton; New York: Knopf, 2001), 151-52.
8. *Not the Way It's Supposed to Be*, 62.
9. Alan Mann, *Atonement for a 'Sinless' Society* (Milton Keynes, Bucks: Paternoster, 2005), 1-59.
10. "What Is *This Life* For? Expanding our View of Salvation," in *What Does It Mean to Be Saved?* (ed. J. G. Stackhouse, Jr.; Grand Rapids: Baker, 2002), 95, 105.
11. "What Is *This Life* For?" 107.

7. Atoning Moments: Crux Sola?

1. *God So Loved the World* (Grand Rapids: Baker Academic, 2001), 115.
2. I follow here the commentary of Gerhard O. Forde, *On Being a Theologian of the Cross* (Grand Rapids: Eerdmans, 1997). For translations of the *Disputation*, I use *Luther's Works 31: Career of the Reformer: I* (ed. H. J. Grimm; Philadelphia: Fortress, 1957), 35-70.

8. Atoning Moments: Incarnation as Second Adam

1. *Against Heresies*, Preface to Book 5, in *Ante-Nicene Fathers Vol. 1* (ed. Alexander Roberts and James Donaldson; Peabody, Mass.: Hendrickson, 1999), 526.
2. An unparalleled study is D. Boyarin, *Border Lines* (Philadelphia: University of Pennsylvania Press, 2004), 89-111 (also see pp. 112-47).
3. *Border Lines*, 104.
4. See D. A. Carson, "The Vindication of Imputation," in *Justification* (ed. M. Husbands and D. J. Treier; Downers Grove, Ill.: IVP, 2004), 72.
5. *Institutes of the Christian Religion* (ed. John T. McNeill; trans. Ford Lewis Battles; Louisville: Westminster John Knox, 1960), 737.

9. Atoning Moments: Crucifixion

1. *The Cross of Christ*, 68.
2. J. Moltmann, *The Way of Jesus Christ* (Minneapolis: Fortress, 1993), 151.
3. *Four Quartets* (London: Faber and Faber, 1944), 21.

4. It goes without saying that we don't have enough space for anything like an adequate treatment of this most important text. For further discussion, I recommend N. T. Wright, "Romans," in *The New Interpreter's Bible* (ed. L. E. Keck et al.; Nashville: Abingdon, 2002), 468-78; J. D. G. Dunn, *Romans* (WBC 38A; Dallas: Word, 1988), 161-83; D. J. Moo, *The Epistle to the Romans* (NICNT; Grand Rapids: Eerdmans, 1996), 218-43. See also the fine sweep of history in M. Reasoner, *Romans in Full Circle* (Louisville: Westminster John Knox, 2005), 23-41.

5. As it is inaccurate to divorce "declared right" from "making right," so it is inaccurate to see this "right-making" as anything other than God's right-making through Christ's righteousness.

6. See Reasoner, 23-24.

7. J. D. G. Dunn, *Romans*, 166-67.

8. For discussions, see from the traditionalist side M. Husbands and D. J. Treier, *Justification* (Downers Grove, Ill.: IVP, 2004); from the New Perspective side see N. T. Wright, *What Did Saint Paul Really Say?* (Grand Rapids: Eerdmans, 2002), 95-133; J. D. G. Dunn and Alan M. Suggate, *The Justice of God* (Grand Rapids: Eerdmans, 1994).

9. It is not without importance here that we need to distinguish between "envy" (desiring what another has) and "jealousy" (protecting what one has oneself). To speak of God's jealousy is to speak of God's desire to protect his own glory and his jealous protection of that glory.

10. His classical study is "Atonement," in his *The Bible and the Greeks* (London: Hodder & Stoughton, 1935), 82-95; see also his *The Epistle of Paul to the Romans* (London: Hodder and Stoughton, 1932), 20-24; see also A. T. Hanson, *The Wrath of the Lamb* (London: SPCK, 1957). This view was put to a withering critique by L. L. Morris, *The Apostolic Preaching of the Cross*.

11. "Romans," 431.

12. *Past Event and Present Salvation*, 93, 133.

10. Atoning Moments: Easter and Pentecost

1. *A Theology of the New Testament* (rev. ed.; Grand Rapids: Eerdmans, 1993), 352-53.

2. *God So Loved the World*, 97.

3. For the peculiar grammar, see N. T. Wright, *Romans*, 503-4; D. J. Moo, *Romans*, 288-89.

4. On the ascension, a uniformly neglected theme, see P. Toon, *The Ascension of Our Lord* (Nashville: Nelson, 1984), and now D. Farrow, "Ascension," in *Dictionary for Theological Interpretation of the Bible* (ed. K. J. Vanhoozer; Grand Rapids: Baker, 2005), 65-68.

5. For my sketch of the origin of this theme in early Christian thinking, see "Covenant and Spirit: The Origins of the New Covenant Hermeneutic," in *The*

Holy Spirit and Christian Origins (ed. G. N. Stanton, B. W. Longenecker, and S. C. Barton; Grand Rapids: Eerdmans, 2004), 41-54; see also a longer version in *Jesus and His Death* (Waco, Tex.: Baylor University Press, 2005), 293-321.

6. I cannot help but mention Anthony Smith, who blogs at http://post modernnegro.wordpress.com, for his exceptional paper given at a conference at Cornerstone University in the fall of 2005 called "Practicing Pentecost."

7. Put simply, the apocalyptic language from Joel found at Acts 2:19-21 is not something still to be fulfilled but something fulfilled right then, and the language is the language of stripping unjust powers from their thrones of might—in other words, we are right back to the Magnificat of Mary and the woes of Jesus. For discussions, see S. McKnight, *A New Vision for Israel*, 133-49. I draw here on the work of G. B. Caird, R. T. France, and N. T. Wright.

8. *Simply Christian* (San Francisco: HarperSanFrancisco, 2006), 122.

9. *The Way of Jesus Christ*, 185.

11. The Story of Jesus: Passover

1. *The Shape of Soteriology* (Edinburgh: T & T Clark, 1992), 8.

2. Waco, Tex.: Baylor University Press, 2005.

3. In the first chapter of my book on this topic, *Jesus and His Death*, I sketch what historical study of Jesus can do and what it can't do. And I believe, as I argued there, that historical study like this is valuable for historians but of very little use for constructing positive Christian theology. My Christian faith is not based on what I can prove about Jesus on the basis of historical methods, which are always limited, but on what God's Spirit has directed the church to understand about Jesus. Christians do not believe Jesus' death is atoning because we can prove he said just that, but because the gospel reveals to the heart that Jesus' death atones. In this book, and in all work I shall do in the future, I make that faith assumption. My own conclusion is that historical Jesus studies cannot take us far enough. As often as not, they take us to dead-end streets.

12. The Story of Paul: In the Courtroom of God

1. "Romans," 471 (in *The New Interpreter's Bible*, vol. 10; Nashville: Abingdon, 2002).

2. For a brief exposition of the New Perspective, see my essay "The Ego and I: Galatians 2:19 in New Perspective," *Word and World* 20 (2000): 272-80. For fuller analysis, see B. N. Fisk, "Paul: Life and Letters," in *The Face of New Testament Studies* (ed. S. McKnight and G. R. Osborne; Grand Rapids: Baker, 2004), 283-325; and J. D. G. Dunn, "Paul's Theology," in the same volume, pp.

326-48. A complete study can be found in S. Westerholm, *Perspectives Old and New on Paul* (Grand Rapids: Eerdmans, 2004).

3. *Mere Christianity* (New York: Macmillan, 1956), 156.

4. The essay was originally published in the April 2001 issue of *Bible Review*. I quote from the internet edition (p. 3). See http://www.thepaulpage.com/Shape.html. Italics are original.

5. The New Perspective has been criticized for its lack of sensitivity to the mechanics of atonement and justification—in particular, its insensitivity to the significance of double imputation. See Simon Gathercole, *Where Is Boasting?* (Grand Rapids: Eerdmans, 2002); but see now Brian Vickers, *Jesus' Blood and Righteousness* (Wheaton: Crossway, 2006).

6. M. Bird, *The Saving Righteousness of God* (Carlisle, UK: Paternoster, 2006), introduction.

7. J. D. G. Dunn, A. M. Suggate, *The Justice of God*, 25.

8. H. Boersma, *Violence, Hospitality, and the Cross*, 163-64.

9. *Past Event and Present Salvation*, 83, 84, 172-73.

10. J. D. G. Dunn, A. M. Suggate, *The Justice of God*, 8-9.

11. See D. A. Carson, "The Vindication of Imputation: On Fields of Discourse and Semantic Fields," in *Justification* (ed. M. Husbands and D. J. Treier; Downers Grove, Ill.: IVP, 2004), 71-78, but the oddity of this discussion of "union with Christ" as the ground of justification is precisely what the Eastern Orthodox do argue, and Carson maintains that *theosis* sacrifices the Reformation understanding of justification. I see a major critique of this conclusion of Carson by McCormack's article, which follows Carson's (see p. 107; McCormack contends that a truly consistent Reformation view of justification is that it precedes "union with Christ").

12. D. J. Moo, *Romans*, 377.

13. See S. Gathercole, "The Doctrine of Justification in Paul and Beyond," in *Justification in Perspective* (ed. B. L. McCormack; Grand Rapids: Baker Academic, 2006), 225-29.

13. The Story of Early Theologians: Irenaeus and Athanasius

1. *Against Heresies* 5.21.1, in *Ante-Nicene Fathers Vol. 1* (ed. Alexander Roberts and James Donaldson; Peabody, Mass.: Hendrickson, 1999), 548-49.

2. *Incarnation of the Word* 54.3, in *Nicene and Post-Nicene Fathers Vol. 4* (Second series; ed. Philip Schaff and Henry Wace; Grand Rapids: Eerdmans, 1953), 65.

3. *Incarnation of the Word* 6.1 (p. 39).

4. *Incarnation of the Word* 8.2, 4 (p. 40).

5. *Against Heresies* 3.18.7 (p. 448).

6. "The Earliest Patristic Interpretations of Psalm 82, Jewish Antecedents, and the Origin of Christian Deification," *JTS* 56 (2005): 30-74.

7. *Against Heresies* 3.18.7 (p. 448).
8. *Against Heresies* 5.1.1 (p. 527).
9. G. Florovsky, *Creation and Redemption* (Belmont, Mass.: Nordland, 1976), 98.
10. Online at http://home.it.net.au/~jgrapsas/pages/sermon.htm. Accessed April 19, 2007.

14. Which Is the Fairest of Them All?

1. *Free of Charge*, 145.
2. See F. LeRon Shults, *Reforming the Doctrine of God* (Grand Rapids: Eerdmans, 2005), 205-34.

15. Atonement as Missional Praxis: Fellowship

1. *Good News and Good Works* (Grand Rapids: Baker, 1993), 76.
2. See his *Reforming Theological Anthropology* (Grand Rapids: Eerdmans, 2003).
3. *The Faces of Forgiveness*, 156-61.
4. *Seek the Welfare of the City* (Grand Rapids: Eerdmans, 1994), 37.

16. Atonement as Missional Praxis: Justice

1. *A Theology for the Social Gospel* (Louisville: Westminster John Knox, 1997), 1, 5.
2. On this, see S. Hauerwas, "The Christian Difference: Or, Surviving Postmodernism," in his *A Better Hope* (Grand Rapids: Brazos, 2000), 35-46.
3. *Foolishness to the Greeks* (Grand Rapids: Eerdmans, 1986), 37.
4. The verse is full of puns: "And he hoped for *mishpat*, and there came *mispah* [uncertain meaning]; he hoped for *tsedeqah*, and there came *tse'aqah* [outcry]."
5. *Exclusion and Embrace* (Nashville: Abingdon, 1996), 29.
6. F. LeRon Shults, *The Faces of Forgiveness*; M. Volf, *Exclusion and Embrace*; C. Marshall, *Beyond Retribution: A New Testament Vision for Justice, Crime, and Punishment* (Grand Rapids: Eerdmans, 2001).
7. *Exclusion and Embrace*, 225.

17. Atonement as Missional Praxis: Missional

1. *Emerging Churches* (Grand Rapids: Baker, 2005), 134.
2. Brian McLaren, *A Generous Orthodoxy* (Grand Rapids: Zondervan, 2004), 105.

3. David J. Bosch, *Transforming Mission*; L. Newbigin, *The Gospel in a Pluralist Society* (Grand Rapids: Eerdmans, 1989); *The Open Secret* (rev. ed.; Grand Rapids: Eerdmans, 1995).

4. *Transforming Mission*, 10.

5. *A Generous Orthodoxy*, 108.

6. *Letters and Papers from Prison* (enl. ed.; ed. E. Bethge; New York: Macmillan, 1971), 382-83.

7. I use the terms found in D. L. Guder, ed., *Missional Church* (Grand Rapids: Eerdmans, 1998), 190-98.

8. Bruce Winter, *Seek the Welfare of the City*, 42.

9. *Transforming Mission*, 420.

18. Atonement as Missional Praxis: Living the Story of the Word

1. *On Christian Doctrine* (trans. D. W. Robertson; New York: The Liberal Arts Press, 1958), 30-31.

2. *Eat This Book* (Grand Rapids: Eerdmans, 2006).

3. John Goldingay, *Models of Scripture* (Grand Rapids: Eerdmans, 1994), 10.

4. Telford Work, *Living and Active* (Grand Rapids: Eerdmans, 2002), 316.

5. Jean W. Cash, *Flannery O'Connor: A Life* (Knoxville: The University of Tennessee, 2002).

6. See *Eat This Book*, 31-35.

7. On this, see the excellent commentary by Phil Towner, *1 and 2 Timothy and Titus* (Grand Rapids: Eerdmans, 2006), 580-94.

8. T. Work, *Living and Active*, 9.

19. Atonement as Missional Praxis: Baptism, Eucharist, and Prayer

1. *The Story of Atonement* (London: Darton, Longman, and Todd, 1997), 126-27.

2. Josephus, *Jewish Antiquities Books XVIII-XX* (trans. Louis H. Feldman; Cambridge, Mass.: Harvard University Press, 1965), 81, 83.

3. G. Theissen, *The Social Setting of Pauline Christianity* (Philadelphia: Fortress, 1989).

4. *Praying with the Church* (Brewster, Mass.: Paraclete, 2006).

SUBJECT INDEX

I express my gratitude here to Hauna Ondrey for compiling these indices.

Abelard, 114
Anselm, 66, 108, 111
Aristotle, 18
Athanasius, 99, 100, 101, 102, 110
Atonement, theories of, 39-43
Augustine, 48, 142, 145
Aulén, Gustaf, 110

Bacote, Vincent, 49
Baker, Mark, 40
Baptism, 149-52
Barth, Karl, 20
Benedict, Saint, 156
Berdyaev, Nicolai, 20
Berlin, Isaiah, 35
Bibliolatry, 143
Biddle, Mark, 23, 47
Bird, Michael, 94
Blount, Brian, 44
Boersma, Hans, 39, 95
Bolger, Ryan, 134
Bonhoeffer, Dietrich, 135
Bosch, David, 2, 135, 141
Boyarin, Daniel, 56
Brunner, Emil, 23

Caird, G. B., 36
Calvin, John, 60, 93
Carson, D. A., 40, 59, 97

Cash, Jean, 144
Christus Victor, 70-73, 104-5, 110-11
Chrysostom, John, 105
Church, 25-31, 73-78, 92-95, 119-23, 128-31, 136-37, 145-46, 151-53
Confucius, 18
Corcoran, Kevin, 46
Cross, 51-53, 61-69

Darwin, 18
Death, 15, 72-73, 102-3, 113
Divine child abuse, 40-41
Dodd, C. H., 67
Dunn, James D. G., 65, 91, 95, 96

Edwards, Jonathan, 41
Eikon. See Image of God
Eternity, 25-27
Eucharist, 152-54
Evangelism, 134-41
Exemplarism, 114-15

Fellowship, 119-23
Fiddes, Paul, 25, 68, 95, 114
Florovsky, Georges, 104
Forgiveness, 29-30
Freud, Sigmund, 18

Gibbs, Eddie, 134
Goldingay, John, 142
Green, Joel, 40

SCRIPTURE INDEX